The Contracting State

Studies in Law and Politics

Published by Open University Press in association with the
Centre for Socio-Legal Studies

Published Titles

Patrick Birkinshaw	*Reforming the Secret State*
Norman Lewis (ed)	*Happy and Glorious:*
	The Constitution in Transition
Michael Purdue	*Planning Appeals: A Critique*
Norman Lewis	*Inner City Regeneration:*
	The Demise of Regional and Local Government
Ian Harden	*The Contracting State*

The Contracting State

by

Ian Harden

Edited by

Norman Lewis and Cosmo Graham

Open University Press
Buckingham - Philadelphia

Open University Press
Celtic Court
22 Ballmoor
Buckingham MK18 1XW

and

1900 Frost Road, Suite 101
Bristol, PA 19007, USA

First Published 1992

A catalogue record of this book is available from the British Library.

Library of Congress Cataloging in Publication Data
 Harden, Ian.
The Contracting State / Ian Harden
p. cm. -- (Studies in Law and Politics)
ISBN 0-335-09634-4 (pbk.)
1. Public contracts -- Great Britain. 2. Municipal Services -- Law
and Legislation -- Great Britain. I. Title. II. Series.
KD1611.H37 1992
346.41'023 -- dc20
[344.10623]

91-45164
CIP

Printed in Great Britain by J.W. Arrowsmith Limited, Bristol.

Contents

Acknowledgements

This book has been much influenced by a Centre for Socio-Legal Studies research programme on markets, citizenship and regulation. I owe a particular debt to Norman Lewis and Di Longley, who willingly shared their research materials and ideas (on 'Next Steps' and the NHS respectively) with me. Special thanks are also due to Roger Brownsword, Cosmo Graham and Mark Stephens. I would also like to record my gratitude to the Department of Law Research Fund for its generous support.

Editorial Introduction

A glance at the title of this piece might deceive a casual reader about its contents. *The Contracting State* conjures up images of public procurement, of the mass purchase of everything from paper clips to Trident submarines. Interesting and controversial as an examination of such issues might be, the present piece casts its net much wider. It is examining nothing less than what might, in the future, be seen as fundamental attempts to re-organise the structures of our public institutions.

Such attempts, the examples in this piece being the re-organisation of the NHS, competitive tendering for local authorities and the 'next steps' agencies, are often described under the rubric of 'contract' and 'competition'. In one sense, they can be seen as developing from the rhetoric of 'rolling back the state' employed by Mrs Thatcher's governments. How better to deal with the inefficiencies of state bureaucracies than to introduce the rigours of private sector contracting? How better to make these bureaucracies more accountable to their customers than by giving the customers legally enforceable rights, such as they would have in the normal contractual situation? The contract state, in this interpretation, is the minimal state, one where the local authorities meet once a year to award the relevant contracts, have lunch and go home, happy in a job well done. In another sense, it is the state of the Citizen's Charter, where citizens know their rights and entitlements and can obtain redress for breaches of such entitlements.

As Ian Harden demonstrates in this piece, reality is more complex. He argues forcefully that the notion of contracts between public bodies is a development which must be seen and assessed independently of its origins in a particular political programme. The nub of the idea, he argues, is about structuring and confining discretion. Thus, for example, by separating purchaser and provider functions in the NHS, institutions with separate interests are created who will each have their own motivations for reducing the discretion of the other. Setting out their obligations in a 'contract' is simply a device for making it clearer what those respective rights and duties are. In other words, this is a modern version of the separation of powers doctrine, but instead of distinguishing between legislative, executive and judicial functions, it concentrates on separating out purchaser and provider functions.

The problem is, as Ian Harden argues, that the idea of a 'contract' cannot, of itself, resolve the problems of discretion and accountability. Thus, for example, the framework documents which set out the relationships between 'next steps' agencies and their responsible departments cannot have contractual status, in the sense of being legally binding, because the agencies do not have a legal personality separate from that of the departments. The only sanction for breach of such agreement is ministerial responsibility to Parliament, a hollow vessel. What is needed to fulfil the rhetorical promises of contract, he argues, is to produce new institutions and doctrines which break from our classical constitutional assumptions. Thus we need some notion of a 'public law contract' with its own principles regarding formation, pricing and dispute-resolution because relationships between such organisations often depend on shared values and interests which cannot be defined in purely commercial terms. The decision-making processes surrounding such a contract must be open and accountable through, at a minimum, the publication of such contracts, as well as providing means for the input of interested parties. To an extent, as Ian Harden points out, these issues can no longer be avoided because of the European Community rules on public procurement.

All our discussion so far has centred around the difficulty of establishing relationships between public bodies and nothing has been said about the rights of the consumer, or citizen, or customer? As is argued, citizen, customer and consumer mean different things and imply different levels of entitlement. However we classify people, the notion of purchaser/provider contracts has no necessary implications for their rights. One technique of trying to make these contracts effective is to give consumers enforceable rights, but as he argues, this will require a new approach as our existing rules relating to consumer rights, for example, in relation to public utilities, are woefully deficient. Providing such rights is a central theme of the Citizen's Charter but, although full of good intentions, the development of the Chartermark standard and the procedures for its award, remain to be fleshed out.

What can be seen from these descriptions is that the new approaches are raising old problems, albeit in fresh guises. A clear lesson of the piece is that there are no easy answers as regards reform of our governing institutions. Instead we must return to first principles, to establishing the values that guide our constitutional framework and seeking to develop institutions which can put those values into operation. The notion of contract is clearly one such idea but it needs to be placed on a firm constitutional footing. It cannot provide that footing in and of itself.

CODA

This is the last in the series *Studies in Law and Politics*. The success of this series has led us to embark on a new series of more substantial books entitled *Law and Political Change*, which will also be published by the Open University Press. Like *Studies in Law and Politics*, but with a broader scope, this series will publish books at the interface of law and politics, with the emphasis on contributions to political debate and the process of political change. Further details are available from the editors (at the address below) or from the Open University Press.

In working on *Studies in Law and Politics* we have incurred numerous debts, which need acknowledgement. First and foremost, we owe a deep debt of gratitude to Julie Prescott, the Series secretary, who struggled valiantly with temperamental hardware and software, as well as conflicting and obscure instructions from the Editors, all with good humour and exemplary efficiency. Secondly, we would like to thank the contributors to the Series for the high quality of their contributions and the good humour with which they tolerated our editorial intrusions. We also owe a debt of gratitude to all our colleagues in the Centre for Socio-Legal Studies who supported us in their varying ways. Last, but not least, we gratefully acknowledge the financial support of the Department of Law, University of Sheffield.

Cosmo Graham and Norman Lewis
Centre for Socio-Legal Studies
University of Sheffield

Introduction

In the 1980s, discussion of the public sector focussed on privatisation and the search for economy and efficiency. The 1990s promise to be the decade of public services. 'Contract' has become a key aspect of the debate. The Citizen's Charter (Cm 1599) draws on the 'customer contracts' pioneered by local government. Large-scale contracting out of services to the private sector was recommended by a Treasury study in the mid-1980s (Treasury 1986) and has already become a partial reality in both local and central government. Contract plays a key role in reforms both of the National Health Service and of training provision through Training and Enterprise Councils. A parliamentary select committee recommended that 'framework documents' governing relations between 'Next Steps' executive agencies and ministers should be regarded as contracts (Treasury and Civil Service Committee 1988). The General Director of the Institute of Economic Affairs has even called for a 'contract state', in which government itself is conceived as being 'a series of contracts' (Mather 1991).

There is nothing new in the public procurement of goods, or the carrying out of public works, by contract. Contract can also be used to procure public services. However, there is no easy answer to the question of what exactly a 'public service' is. In a preliminary way, two categories can be identified (Marlin 1984): services performed directly for citizens (like refuse collection); or indirectly, to support government operations (such as maintenance of the vehicles in which the refuse is collected). The main focus of this book is on direct services. Contractual procurement of indirect services is important and its extension is a significant element of government policy in favour of contracting out. Furthermore the direct/indirect distinction is not watertight (consider hospital cleaning, for example). However, many indirect services have always been procured through contract and close analogies can be drawn with the 'core business' approach of the private sector, in which companies focus on the activity which they can do best and buy support services from outside suppliers (see e.g. CBI 1988).

In contrast, widespread use of contract in the organization of direct public services is relatively new in contemporary Britain (though 'farming out' the care of pauper children, for example, was a common nineteenth century practice). To survey the whole field of direct services would be beyond the scope of a work of this size. Attention is therefore focussed on three areas which together illustrate the range of issues: the NHS, local authority services subject to compulsory competitive tendering and 'Next Steps' agencies.

The central argument of the book is that the use of contract in public services has two aspects. One is the pursuit of specific political objectives. In relation to these, the language of contract has a largely ideological significance. 'Contract' connotes individual rights and freedom of choice. It is also essential to the functioning of the market system. Hence it is associated with consumer sovereignty over decisions about what shall be produced and with efficiency in the process of supply. These are things that are of fundamental importance in terms of constitutional values. However, 'contract' does not refer to a clear legal framework which can be applied directly, or by analogy, so as to realize them in the context of public services.

In contrast, the other aspect of the contractual approach is a genuine potential for promoting constitutional values through an institutional separation of functions. Specifically, responsibility for deciding what services there shall be is distinguished from responsibility for delivering the services. This separation of the roles of 'purchaser' and 'provider' offers the opportunity not only to pursue economy, efficiency and effectiveness, but also to enhance both individual rights and the accountability of government for policy decisions. However, the contractual approach cannot bring about these results by itself. It can do so only as part of a broader legal and constitutional framework for public services which, at present, does not exist. The ambiguity of the book's title reflects the danger that results. Without an appropriate framework, the contractual approach

may lead to a contraction of public services, or to a loss of their 'public' aspect.

Chapter 1 discusses the values which underlie the attractiveness of contract as a symbol. Freedom of contract and the legally binding quality of contractual rights are identified as essential aspects of the rule of law. Consumer sovereignty is presented as a form of democratic control over decision-making, based on - and supporting - individual autonomy. Chapter 2 focusses on the nature of individual rights in relation to public services and on the concept of public service itself. Chapter 3 describes the new structures that have been established in the three areas chosen for study and their intended purpose of improving management through the separation of purchaser and provider functions. Chapter 4 discusses how the contractual approach is supposed to work and identifies its institutional - and constitutional - implications.

Chapter 5 examines the legal framework through which the changes in these fields actually operate. In practice, the ordinary law of contract plays only a limited role. Neither the contracting out of direct services, nor their re-organization so as to separate purchaser and provider functions within the public sector, alters the legal basis on which individuals receive public services. The impact of European Community law is discussed in Chapter 6. Chapter 7 considers the issues of quality and performance in contracts for public services and their relationship to questions, more familiar to lawyers, about the control of administrative discretion.

Finally, Chapter 8 sets out an agenda for legal and constitutional change to ensure that, so far as possible, the aspirations of contract identified in Chapter 1 are realised in the field of public services. If the separation of purchaser and provider functions is to lead to greater accountability and more rights for individuals, then there needs to be a secure legal basis for organizational independence in the public sector, compatible with the concept of 'public service'. In other words, there must be some alternative, other than the model of the commercial company, to the all-pervasive grip of ministerial responsibility over the public sector. This means using procedures that are open and accountable as a way of justifying the various levels of decision that make up the effective demand for a public service. There is also need for a new legal mechanism - a 'public law contract' - that would require the substantive question of why a service is public to be addressed by those responsible for 'purchasing' decisions.

Chapter 1

The Moral Promise of Contract

'Contract' is a term with a specific legal meaning. It is also pregnant with social, economic and political significance. When local councils publish 'contracts' for the 'customers' of their services, for example, appeal is made to a powerful symbol. In this chapter, the moral promise of that symbol will be analysed. The purpose is to examine the ideals which underlie the apparent attractiveness of 'contract' as a model to which public services should aspire.

During the 19th century the principles of the law of contract were systematically developed in a way which partly reflected the intellectual success of liberal economic ideas. The classical liberal market economy is one of private economic actors. The role of government is not to be a player in the market, but to provide a framework for it to function. A necessary element of the framework is the law of contract, which makes it possible for people to undertake legally binding obligations towards one another. This facilitates the trust and confidence necessary for voluntary transactions between those who own, or control, resources of various kinds.

In a market economy, demand for goods and services and their supply are linked automatically, by flows of expenditure and income through voluntary, contractual, channels. Demand is the aggregate of individual spending decisions. Productive resources are allocated amongst suppliers on the basis of their efficiency and effectiveness in meeting such demand. Distribution of the final product follows demand. The engine of the system is the pursuit of self-interest. The steering is provided by the price mechanism. Social goals - what to produce, how to produce it and how it should be distributed - are not the subject of authoritative decision, but result automatically from the market's aggregation of individual choices. Since market actors are assumed to operate in a rational, self-interested way, the key variable in the system is provided by the preferences of consumers. In other words; consumers are sovereign.

Consumer sovereignty links the economic aspects of the market with a set of moral commitments. The market provides a model of economic efficiency, in which no more wants can be satisfied without some sacrifice of other wants. It also embodies values of equality and freedom. Individuals are free to express their wishes through market choices. They can buy what they want and reject ('exit' from) what they do not. The market is no respecter of status. All effective demand counts equally. Consumer sovereignty thus amounts to a version of democratic equality in the process of determining economic outcomes; 'voice' as well as 'exit' (Hirschman 1970). In a well-functioning market, no single individual's decision to buy or refrain from buying can affect prices and so alter signals to producers as to what should be supplied. Consumer sovereignty is collective sovereignty, albeit founded on individual autonomy.

The relationship is reciprocal. Consumer sovereignty also contributes to individual autonomy. In a market economy, individuals' livelihoods are not dependent on other people's valuation of their merit. It is sufficient to be able to perform some work, or sell a service, for which there is a demand (Brittan and Webb 1990). For those who can do so, consumer sovereignty thus provides the material underpinning necessary for individuals to make use of their freedom from interference by others.

These values of equality and freedom, although emphasised by Hayek, have often been neglected in debates about the market. Such debates tend to focus either on questions of economics, or on issues of distributional equity about which the market model is notoriously silent. By contrast, the law of contract has always had an overtly moral flavour. The key principle is 'freedom of contract'. Although this now tends to be understood exclusively in terms of nineteenth century liberal political economy, its roots go much deeper.

Freedom of Contract

The most obvious meaning of the principle is that the parties to a contract are free to reach what bargain they please. Legal rules about contracts are power-conferring (Hart 1961). They enable individuals to create, vary and destroy legal rights and obligations, through voluntary transactions with others. The validity of such transactions is not, in general, subject to the permission or approval of governments. On the contrary, the state is bound by the use which individuals together choose to make of the powers conferred by the law of contract. Contractual rights are legal rights, which the courts have an obligation to uphold, just as they do Acts of Parliament.

Contract thus enables the participants in private social relations to give legal validity to rules which they voluntarily accept for their own self-government. From this perspective, freedom of contract is a 'positive' not a 'negative' freedom (Berlin 1969: 131). However, it would be inconsistent with the liberal notion of the autonomy of the individual, which underlies this positive freedom, for it to become the basis for its own destruction. Hence there are individual rights which are literally inalienable. A contract by which A agrees to become B's slave, for example, is void.

Equally significant is that individuals are entitled to refuse to enter into a contract, no matter how great the status or power of the would-be contractual partner. Here freedom and equality are inextricably mingled together. Historically, the establishment of freedom of contract meant limiting the personal submission, characteristic of feudal social relations, of one individual to another. This 'depersonalization' of power (Poggi 1978) was fundamental to the emergence of the rule of law as a principle governing the public sphere of relationships between individuals and the state. If a contract is not performed, the aggrieved party has the right to call on the state to enforce the obligation (Collins 1986). The right not to enter a contract is thus an essential aspect of the rule of law. Without it, the weak would be exposed to the arbitrary and compulsory imposition of obligations by the strong, who would then receive the backing of the state to enforce them.

The Binding Nature of Contractual Obligations

The rule of law is also implicated when an individual seeks a remedy for breach of contract. The individual appears before the court to invoke the assistance of the state not as a supplicant, but as the possessor of a legal right. If the contract itself is with a state body, the empowerment of the individual is even more marked. There is not a mere hope of receiving some benefit, dependent on the exercise of discretionary powers, but a legal entitlement. The binding nature of contractual obligations *vis-a-vis* the organs of the state is also essential in enabling the individual to enjoy economic security and the independence which this permits, both of the state and of other individuals. Because they are binding, contractual rights are the functional equivalent of property rights and have the same mixed political, social and economic significance.

Freedom of contract and the legally binding quality of contractual obligations together amount to a particular conception of individual autonomy, both in relations with the state and with other members of civil society. Despite this, it is easy to overlook the historical and conceptual links between contract and citizenship, because the law of contract developed separately from public law, particularly in the nineteenth century. In the Anglo-American legal tradition, contract has come to be thought of as quintessentially private law, separate and distinct from the law governing relations between the individual and the state. However, the conceptual divide between 'public' and 'private' has now ceased to correspond to the way the world actually works. Legal structures and ways of thought need to be re-adapted accordingly (Birkinshaw et al 1990; Mather 1991: 13-15).

The Bureaucratization of Contract

Organizations - particularly companies - play a fundamental role in the modern economy. This complicates the model of contract as bargained transactions between individuals. The individual entering a contract with an organization tends to be faced with a 'standard form'; a set of rules which must be accepted or declined as a whole. The terms of such contracts closely resemble the administrative rules of a public body to which an individual may apply for a grant, licence or other benefit.

Standard forms present two challenges to the moral basis of contract. Firstly, as with inalienable rights, it is necessary to prevent contract from becoming the means of its own negation. This happens if standard terms exclude liability for contractual non-performance, or for loss caused through for example, negligence. If uncontrolled, the freedom of contract enjoyed by organizations to use exclusion clauses threatens the bindingness of contractual obligations and the security for individual autonomy offered by other civil law rights.

Recognition of this fact gave a major impetus to the development of a 'consumer-welfarist' element in English contract law, stressing elements such as reasonableness and fair-dealing. This approach competes with a continuing 'market-individualism' which seeks to uphold the terms of contracts into which people have entered, unless their consent is vitiated by fraud, mistake, or duress (Adams and Brownsword 1987; Brownsword 1989). As regards the standard terms on which individuals deal with organizations, however, the need for regulation by public authority in order to protect the core contractual value of individual autonomy has been largely conceded in principle.

The second challenge to the moral basis of contract posed by standard forms is that they violate the individualist assumption that the terms of a contract are freely negotiated. The element of voluntariness is reduced, even in principle, to the decision whether or not to enter the contract. Consumer sovereignty, however, offers a re-interpretation of the significance of individual freedom of contract. Even if it is no longer possible to bargain with an organization, freedom of contract ensures democratic equality in economic decision-making and responsiveness of producer organizations to the range of variation within aggregate consumer choice. Individuals can thus participate in a collective decision as to what should be produced by enjoying, as individual consumers, the maximum choice that is economically feasible.

The moral promise of contract is thus a complex mixture of elements. There is individual autonomy. This is partly embodied in the binding quality of contractual obligations, which means the individual is dependent neither on other people, nor on the discretionary power of the state. Individual autonomy is also partly about choice; not freedom to bargain necessarily, but freedom to choose between the range of goods and services whose production is determined by consumer sovereignty. Consumer sovereignty thus also offers the promise of a kind of democratic equality in economic decision-making; collective 'voice' through individual decisions to pay for some things and not for others.

In the next chapter it will be argued that contract does not offer a straightforward model of how these important values can be realized in the context of public services. Individuals relate to public services not just in one way, as consumers, but also as citizens and customers. Nor do these roles correspond directly to the different ways in which public services may be financed.

Chapter 2

Consumers, Citizens and Customers

The word 'customer' is a very dangerous and difficult word to use in the context of public service.
(Sir Peter Kemp, in evidence to the Public Accounts Committee, 38th Report, HC 420 1988/89).

Contract provides a mechanism by which the supply of *private* services can be organized through the market. In so doing, it binds together individual legal rights and consumer sovereignty. The way in which private services are funded (i.e., by payments from those who choose to receive them) resolves questions about what should be supplied and about who should get what. This chapter will argue that contract cannot work the same magic for public services. The crucial issue turns out to be not how public services are paid for, but whether there is an authoritative public decision that a service should exist.

In the absence of consumer sovereignty over this question, the links between the 'demand' for public services, their supply and the rights of individuals become complex and contingent. The nature of these links is explored in the second part of the chapter. It will be argued that there is scope for increasing the responsiveness of public services to various forms of expression of consumer demand. However, the 'public' nature of public services means that they must be responsive not only to individuals as consumers, but also to citizens and customers. Greater individual legal rights to public services are valuable in themselves and also promote the effective supply of public services. However, they do not empower individuals in relation to decisions about the kind or level of public services that should be provided.

Charges, Prices and Taxes

A contract for public services clearly does not result in consumer sovereignty when it is between the provider of the service and a public body; as, for example, when a local authority contracts to have the streets cleaned. In this case, the ultimate consumers of the service are not the 'customer' under the contract. 'Demand' for the service is established by public decision, not by the aggregation of consumer preferences. It makes no difference whether the body which provides the public service under contract is itself public or private.

That 'demand' is established by authoritative public decision is - to a greater or lesser extent - the case for all public services, not just those where there is a contract between the provider and a public purchaser. This is true whether or not the service is provided free at the point of consumption. Charges may be levied on the consumers of public services, but for there to be a market governed by consumer sovereignty, services must be *priced*.

Charges, or 'user fees' as they are referred to in the American literature, differ from prices along two dimensions. Firstly, they are not necessarily set by market forces, but may be authoritatively determined. They may fail to cover, just cover, or more than cover, the costs of providing the service. Secondly, charges may be made compulsory, in that the duty to pay does not arise from any individual choice to receive the service in question. This may be because the law makes the service obligatory (like school education) or because, by its nature, the service cannot be restricted to, or rejected by, particular individuals (e.g., street-cleaning). Other charges relate to public services which individuals choose to consume in the same way that they do private services (e.g., museum entrance fees). Charges may also be made for 'services' which an individual would not purchase in a free market, but which public authority imposes as a precondition for engaging in an activity which the individual wishes to perform (e.g., licences). In brief, charges occupy the ground that separates taxes from prices.

English courts have distinguished a charge from a tax on the basis that the former must relate to services which confer a benefit on the person paying, as distinct from that conferred on the public generally

(*Daymond v South West Water Authority* [1976] 1 All ER 39). The United States Supreme Court has held that user fees must meet the same criterion, but must also attach to a voluntary act, such as applying for a licence (*National Cable Television Association v United States* (1974) 415 US 336; *Federal Power Commission v New England Power Co.* (1974) 415 US 345).

However, in respect of services provided by a public body under statutory powers, there is no clear basis in English law for any distinction between a charge and a price. Payments demanded without specific statutory authorization are probably unlawful (c.f. *A-G v Wilts United Dairies Ltd.* (1921) 37 T. L. R. 884). This can be argued in terms of the high constitutional principle, enshrined in the Bill of Rights of 1689, that money cannot be levied without the authority of Parliament. It also has a more mundane rationale. When we are dealing with a service provided by the state, the decision that the service should exist and the question of how it should be paid for (including what role, if any, there should be for charges) are, in fact, separate matters. Public services can always be funded out of general taxation. Hence the power or duty to provide a service is one thing; the power or duty to levy charges another.

What is a Public Service?

Public services may be provided by a private body (as, for example, where a local authority service such as street cleaning is provided by a private company under contract). Provision of a public service may be made conditional upon payment. These two facts together raise the question of how public services are to be distinguished from private ones, since neither the status of the provider, nor the presence or absence of payment by the consumer is decisive. Given the importance of the concept of consumer sovereignty, it is tempting to suggest that a service is 'private' only if there is no form of intervention by public authority in its provision through the market. However, this would mean that there were very few private services since, in practice, almost all services are subject to some degree of regulation.

A more appropriate legal criterion for distinguishing public from private services is whether the existence of the service is a matter for consumer sovereignty in the market, or of authoritative public decision. Judgments about the category into which a service ought to fall are complex, involving debate about economic factors and about individual rights. To develop a concept of public service, these issues must be addressed and it will be argued later that there is no escaping the need for such a concept. However, in marking out the field of enquiry into 'contracts for public services', it is sufficient to focus on the current pattern of public decisions that services should exist.

There are broadly two ways in which public authority may give effect to such a decision (Daintith 1989). The first is by using resources to provide the service. The second is by using the command of law to make provision of the service a public law duty. The two overlap when a public body is placed under a statutory obligation to provide a service, so the command of law only widens the field of public services when duties are imposed on private bodies.

The stipulation that a service is public if its existence is currently mandated by public authority brings three categories within the field of 'public services': (a) services provided by a public body directly; (b) services purchased by a public body through contract; and (c) services which a private body has a public law duty to provide. The latter category includes privatised utilities such as gas, electricity and water.

Individuals and Public Services

If public services are those whose existence is a matter of authoritative public decision, then obviously they cannot be governed wholly by consumer sovereignty expressed through individuals' decisions to buy the service in the marketplace. However, since public services can be charged for, willingness to pay can be used not only as a mechanism of distribution, but also as a source of information about preferences (Rose 1990). For this to be possible, it must be feasible to restrict consumption of the service to those who pay. Furthermore, if willingness to pay is to provide information about demand, the service must be one which individuals actually want (like entrance to a museum, or a supply of electricity) rather than one to which by law they must submit in order to get something they do want (like planning permission). A service that meets both conditions will here be referred to as 'marketable'.

Consumers

Like a private service, a marketable public service has identifiable individual consumers. Not all such services could be provided privately. Registration of patents and trade-marks, for example, depends on the exercise of public authority (although the administrative functions concerned could be delegated to a private company). Nor are all marketable public services actually charged for. In fact, the practice of charging for public services in Britain appears to be inconsistent, illogical and unguided by principle (Rose 1990).

Even if charges are levied, the use which is made of information provided by willingness to pay depends upon how the service is organised. There are many possible gradations in the degree of responsiveness. At one extreme, a public service may be operated on a straightforward commercial basis. At the other, a public service might be (a) marketable and (b) charged for and yet information provided by consumer payments play no role at all in decisions about what service is to be provided. The charge may be used simply as a rationing and/or revenue-raising device.

There may be many good reasons why information provided by consumers' willingness to pay should have either no role, or only a limited role, in decision-making about marketable public services. Some are reasons against charging. Others are arguments against relying, or relying too heavily, on information provided by charges in deciding what the service should be - even though it may be perfectly reasonable to make a charge. It may be thought, for example, that a particular service should be provided free at the point of consumption and/or that it should be compulsory (e.g., health, school education). A service may provide public benefits which go beyond those accruing to the individual consumer (e.g., training, public transport, refuse collection, driving tests - to take a number of examples at random). Furthermore, the distinction between services which people want and those they must have by law as a precondition for something else is not watertight, especially where the service is one which depends on the exercise of public authority (consider, for example, registration of companies).

Citizens

Not all public services are marketable. Those which are not (such as many aspects of policing) by their very nature lack identifiable individual consumers. Nonetheless, it is possible for individual citizens to have rights in respect of such services. For example, they may legitimately expect the police to respond to reports of crimes and to behave in certain ways and not in others (e.g., politely and not aggressively).

A conception of the rights of citizens may be the reason for certain marketable public services not being marketed. If all citizens are thought to be entitled to health care, for example, this may be a good reason for such care being provided free at the point of consumption. In this type of case, the reason why a service is not marketed is because the rights of the citizen as an individual recipient of the service are more, not less important, than in respect of other services. In other cases, services are not marketed because of the public interest in more of the service being provided than individuals would choose, or be able, to afford (e.g., training). However, there is no necessary reason why individual preferences should not count in decisions about such services (as they do where public subsidies are used to raise the level of effective demand for a service). In many cases it may be debatable whether a service is not marketed because of a view about rights, or because of a view about public benefit (e.g., education).

Customers

'Customer' is a slippery term. It is sometimes used to refer to a public body which purchases a service from a provider, sometimes to those here identified as 'consumers'; i.e. the individual recipients of a marketable service. Workers within a single organization have 'internal customers' according to currently fashionable management theories. Like 'client' or 'stakeholder', 'customer' is also used to denote a variety of interests in relation both to services which, though marketable, are not marketed and to those which are non-marketable.

Even in relation to the former, it is often not a simple matter to identify a single consumer or customer. With training, for example, is the customer the trainee, or the actual or potential employer? Both are potential consumers if the service were marketed. In relation to non-marketable services the problem of identification is even worse. Who are the 'customers' of the Benefits Agency, for example? Possible candidates are the recipients of benefits, taxpayers and the government department to which the Agency is responsible.

Consumer, citizen and customer thus represent three overlapping and imprecise ways of expressing categories of legitimate interest in relation to public services. 'Customer' refers not only to individuals, but also to a variety of corporate interests, public and private. 'Consumer' and 'citizen' both refer to individual interests, but no clear difference between them appears in present patterns of usage. All three terms are sometimes used almost interchangeably in discussion of public services (see e.g., Pirie *et al* 1991). This confusion of terminology reflects deeper uncertainties: about which services should be public and why; about how far they should be marketed or charged for; about the nature, scope and purpose of individual rights as regards public services; and about the relationship between these different issues.

Contract and Public Services.

Contract offers a coherent *prima facie* set of answers to equivalent questions about private services. It does so by linking together individual legal rights and consumer sovereignty in the organization of their supply. In relation to public services, the automatic processes of the market are not present. There are no automatic links between the 'demand' for public services, their supply and the rights of individuals. Instead the links are complex and contingent.

In considering how contracts for public services may affect these matters the range of possible contractual relationships needs to be borne in mind:

  (i)   between the individual and a public body which provides a service directly;
  (ii) between the individual and a private body with a public law duty to provide a service.

If a public body obtains a service through contract, there are three further relationships:

  (iii) between the individual and the service provider;
  (iv) between the individual and the public body obtaining the service;
  (v)   between the public body and the service provider.

Creating greater rights for individuals in relationships (i) - (iv) can be understood in terms of one of the core values of the rule of law examined in Chapter 1. That is, that individuals should have legal entitlements rather than be dependent on discretionary decisions by public authority. However, consumers' (or citizens' or customers') rights do not amount to consumer sovereignty.

Traditionally, individuals have a say in determining the content of public services only through politics. The 'demand' for a service - what is to be provided, how much of it and to whom - is established by bureaucratic decisions, for which government is accountable through the electoral system. There is no reason why information concerning individual preferences about public services should not also be obtained through other mechanisms. As we have seen, charges can be used in relation to marketed services. Some such services are already organized on a fully or partially commercial basis. There are also other ways of getting information, applicable to services of all types, such as surveys and feedback from individual complaints into the policy-making process (Lewis *et al* 1987).

Whatever may be thought about the desirability of such developments, their implementation is not a matter of individual rights, but of re-organization of the service concerned to make it responsive to whatever indicator of preferences is to be used. Individual rights in relation to public services and input from individual preferences into decisions about the demand for public services are different things, with different purposes. 'Empowerment' (Pirie *et al* 1991) of individuals through legal rights to public services thus has nothing to do with consumer sovereignty.

On the other hand, individual legal rights can undoubtedly have a direct impact on the supply of public services. Competing suppliers of private services have an economic incentive to provide what is wanted as effectively and efficiently as possible. This is not true of traditional bureaucratic ways of administering public services. As a result, they may be unnecessarily expensive, inefficient and ineffective in achieving their intended goals. Individual legal rights can contribute to the supply-side improvement of public services in respect of the last of these three dimensions. If the goals of a body providing a public service are formulated as legal rights of individuals then there is an extra incentive to attain them. In cases of failure, the provider can ultimately be brought to account through the courts, rather than through the traditional and ineffective channel of redress provided by ministerial responsibility.

However, although individual rights can promote effectiveness, not everything done to improve effectiveness will necessarily enhance individual rights. It will be argued in the next chapter that contracts between a public body and a service provider have to be understood as attempts to improve all three dimensions of the supply of public services. Such contracts do not necessarily create greater rights for individuals (though they may improve the services they receive). Furthermore, 'demand' for the services continues to be set by authoritative public decision.

Chapter 3

The Contractual Approach to Public Services: Three Examples

This chapter examines three areas in which major changes are occuring to the way public services are provided: the National Health Service; compulsory competitive tendering for local authority services and 'Next Steps' agencies. It is not intended to provide a complete explanation of the changes, but rather to draw out the common contractual elements which link developments in the three areas. The first is an institutional separation of the responsibility for deciding what service there shall be from the responsibility for delivering that service. The second is that this division takes the form of an agreed definition of rights and duties, which is intended to be binding, if not necessarily legally enforceable.

In itself, this re-structuring results in an expansion neither of individual legal rights, nor of the role of consumer preferences in decision-making about public services. Its intended effect is to improve the management of public services, though this is intertwined with a number of politically controversial goals. However, it will be argued in Chapter 4 that the contractual approach has a potential constitutional value that is separable from the particular political goals with which its implementation has been connected and which is concealed by the apparently simple notion of 'improved management'.

The NHS Internal Market

Statutory duties to provide, or ensure provision of, health services are imposed on the Secretary of State by the National Health Service Act

1977. Regional and District Health Authorities (RHAs and DHAs) exercise on behalf of the Secretary of State such of his functions as he directs. In addition to DHAs and RHAs, which are statutory corporations, there exist the non-statutory NHS Policy Board and NHS Management Executive (NHSME). The NHSME, headed by the Chief Executive, has terms of reference which include taking central responsibility for the operation and management of the NHS within Ministers' overall policy framework. The Policy Board advises the Secretary of State on policy formulation and strategic oversight of the health service.

The NHS is almost entirely funded from public expenditure. Most NHS services (prescriptions are the main exception) are provided free of charge to the ultimate consumer, including those of general practitioners (GPs) who act as gatekeepers for hospital services. Hitherto, the provision of such services was the direct responsibility of DHAs. The aim of the reforms introduced under the National Health Service and Community Care Act 1990 is to separate the role of the DHA into two separate functions - that of purchaser and provider - and to create an 'internal market' in public health care services. The new system began formal operation in April 1991, but its full impact will take time to emerge.

The concept of an internal market has three interlocking aspects: the creation of incentives to greater efficiency; the delegation of decision-making responsibilities to lower levels; and the principle of money following patients, so as to link resource allocation to service output (Crafts 1989; Hulme 1990). DHAs' primary responsibilities are no longer to provide health services but to assess the health needs of their populations and to arrange for those needs to be met by purchasing services from providers. GPs with larger practices may also become purchasers of services on behalf of their patients. Such 'fund holding' GPs receive directly from the RHA resources which would otherwise have been allocated to the relevant DHA. Although the fact is not emphasised in the official literature, there is no formal barrier to DHAs and GP fund holders purchasing services from private providers, nor to the NHS providing services to private purchasers.

At first, DHAs will continue to have direct management responsibility for most NHS service providers. However, hospital and other units can apply to become NHS Trusts, operationally independent of district and regional management (NHSME 1990a). The key idea of the internal market is that the relationship between a provider - whether a directly managed unit (DMU) or a Trust - and a purchaser (DHA or GP fund holder) should be in the form of a contract which specifies the agreed quality, quantity and cost of services to be provided.

DHAs are expected to wish to secure the maximum volume and quality of health services for their residents at the lowest available cost. Providers are assumed to want to secure the DHA's commitment to funding the maximum use of their facilities, at as good a price as possible, with as little interference in the way in which the service is delivered as possible (NHSME 1990b: para 3.34). The contractual framework of the internal market is supposed to harness these motivations by structuring incentives so as to achieve cost-effectiveness.

Three different types of contract are possible: 'block', 'cost and volume' and 'cost per case' (Department of Health 1989). Cost per case contracts involve *ad hoc* referrals, with the price being fixed on a case-by-case basis and with no prior commitment by either party as to the volume of cases which might be so dealt with. Although an important role was originally envisaged for cost per case contracts, later guidance says that transaction costs make such 'bespoke' contracts for individual patients uneconomic and that their use is likely to be relatively rare (NHSME 1990b: para 3.40).

The block contract involves payment of an annual fee in return for access to a defined range of services and facilities, but with no commitment to a specified volume of output. In essence, this is little different from previous management practice in the NHS. Cost and volume contracts specify outputs, in terms of numbers of patients treated. The form of such contracts favoured by the NHSME (1990b: para 3.39) involves a fixed price up to a volume threshold of treatment and a price per case being paid above the threshold up to a volume ceiling. The intention is that cost and volume contracts should increasingly replace block contracts, thus enabling DHAs to link resource allocation to outputs and providing clear incentives to DMUs and Trusts to improve their efficiency.

The NHS reforms have three aspects. The first is a revised form of NHS management, in which the contractual framework is intended to effect a cultural change towards a focus on outputs, cost-effectiveness and the clear identification of service priorities and requirements. The purchaser role will make DHAs formulate their requirements more clearly and so generate and use the information necessary for that role. Provider units will also need to adopt a similar attitude towards information about their costs. The second element is the integration of private purchasers and providers into a single health care market. Taken by itself, and whilst the obligations of the 1977 Act remain, purchasing and provision of services across the public/private divide is unlikely to alter public health care fundamentally. The sheer financial muscle of public spending on health will ensure that NHS decisions continue to determine the overall pattern of services. However, integration facilitates the marketing of health care services by public providers, particularly if NHS funding leaves them with surplus capacity.

The third element is competition within the NHS itself. Although emphasised in the earlier working documents, this has been down-played more recently, partly for political reasons but also because of the real difficulties it risks creating. Allocation of resources through a competitive market and through management processes structured as contracts are not different versions of the same thing, but fundamentally different processes. The first leads to outcomes which are not planned by anyone. The second is about making the planning process more effective.

A proliferation of GP fund holders and NHS Trusts, making genuinely independent decisions about the purchase and provision of services, would be incompatible with DHA management of health care resources in its area through purchasing. Hence, competition in the NHS is to be 'managed competition' (Appleby et al 1990). Prices, for example, are to reflect costs rather than responding to competitive opportunities (NHSME 1990b: para 4.2). The market players are also subject to discretionary regulation, direction and persuasion from the Department of Health. The Secretary of State has ample statutory powers for this purpose in relation to Trusts. GP fund holders, however, may be a different matter.

Patients will benefit from the changes to the NHS if, whilst other things remain the same, health needs are more accurately identified by DHAs and/or providers become more efficient. However, there is no trace here of greater individual legal rights, nor of the preferences of individual consumers being used to decide what services are provided. At no point do the contracts of the NHS internal market operate with the consumer as the customer. Patients can become agents only by paying for health care privately.

Competitive Tendering and Local Authority Services

This section of the chapter will first examine the concept of competitive tendering and its relationship to contracting out. It then considers compulsory competitive tendering for local authority services.

Competitive tendering occurs when a body which undertakes an activity 'in-house' (i.e., through employing and managing its own staff) invites outside contractors to tender for the work in competition with the in-house unit. The outside contractor could be either a public or a private body, though discussions of competitive tendering by public bodies usually emphasise the role of private contractors. Large-scale competitive tendering for services provided in-house has been promoted by government in the fields of defence (e.g., stores, security functions and facilities management); NHS support services (cleaning, catering and laundry); central government support services and local authority services.

Competitive tendering overlaps with 'contracting out', but is distinct in two ways. Firstly, if the in-house unit wins the competition then the service is not contracted out. 'Market testing' - providing information about market costs and an opportunity to get better value for money either by contracting out, or by improving efficiency in-house - has long been the declared basis of government policy towards competitive tendering (Health Circular 83 (18); Treasury 1986). Secondly, it necessarily involves competition, whereas, in principle, a public body could contract out a service without inviting competitive bids. However, it is general government policy that procurement of goods and services should be competitive (Treasury 1988a). There are also specific legal requirements which will be considered in due course.

The particular context may make competitive tendering a sudden death process for the in-house unit. If it loses the competition, it is broken up and the public body relies henceforth on outside contractors for the service. Competitive tendering may thus be simply a stage on the way to permanent contracting out of a service. Alternatively, the in-house unit may be subject to a more graduated version of market discipline, with the opportunity to improve its performance, though it is in the nature of competitive tendering that failure to compete effectively will sooner or later lead to its demise.

Compulsory Competitive Tendering (CCT)

CCT was first applied to construction and maintenance work carried out by direct labour organizations (Local Government Planning and Land Act 1980) and was phased in for a range of other services under the Local Government Act 1988. The basic principle of the legislation is that competitive tendering is required before a local authority is permitted either to undertake defined categories of work for itself ('functional work'), or to perform work under contract for another authority (under the Local Authorities (Goods and Services) Act 1970). Discussion here will focus on CCT and functional work under the 1988 Act, because some of the services concerned are either direct, or straddle the boundary between direct and indirect services. The Act lists a number of defined activities, with power to add to the list and to provide for exemptions from it, by order (see Table 1, p. 20). In-house units providing such services are known as direct service organizations (DSOs).

The legislation is complex, partly because of the element of compulsion and thus the need to avoid loopholes. What follows is no more than an outline of the main CCT requirements. If an authority intends its DSO to carry out work within a defined activity, it must prepare a detailed specification, advertise the work in a local newspaper and invite expressions of interest in carrying it out. Of those from the private sector who respond, at least three (or all, if there are three or less) must be invited to submit a bid. However, if a large number of contractors respond, four to six should be invited to bid (DoE 1991a: para 28). There must also be a written bid on behalf of the DSO. This may only be accepted in preference to a lower bid if it can be shown that there were sound reasons to justify doing so.

Specification of contract requirements is a complex and difficult task. However, as with NHS contracts, it is the process of specification which requires authorities clearly to identify what it is that they are using public money to provide. In practice, local authorities have been able to do so sufficiently clearly to enable them to use contracts analogous to 'cost and volume contracts' in the health service (Walsh 1991: para 5.15). In carrying out the work, a DSO must comply with the detailed specification for which it bid.

As well as regulating the tendering process itself, the legislation imposes duties on local authorities to keep separate accounts in relation to any work done by a DSO which is subject to competitive tendering. It also gives the Secretary of State power to prescribe financial objectives for an authority in relation to work it undertakes within a defined activity. The effect of these provisions is to enable central government to determine the market performance which DSOs must achieve in order to survive (see DoE 1988: Annex A).

Just as significant, however, is the impact which CCT has on the culture of local authorities. The accounting provisions and financial targets are fundamental to the creation of separate purchaser and provider, or 'client' and 'contractor' roles. The Audit Commission has emphasised the importance of re-designing institutional structures so

Table 1

Services subject to CCT under the Local Government Act 1988*.

(a) Collection of refuse	household and commercial waste.
(b) Cleaning of buildings	interior and window cleaning but not other exterior cleaning.
(c) Other cleaning	removal of litter and emptying of litter bins; street cleaning and gully emptying; cleaning of traffic signs and street name plates.
(d) Catering (education welfare)	providing ingredients for, preparing and delivering and serving meals and providing
(e) other catering	refreshments. Exceptions include delivery (but not preparation) of meals on wheels
(ee) Management of sports and leisure facilities.	
(f) Maintenance of ground	cutting and tending grass; planting and tending trees, hedges, flowers etc.; weed control.
(g) Repair and maintenance of vehicles	excludes accident repairs and maintenance of police and fire service vehicles.

* A local authority is exempted from the CCT requirements in respect of a particular category if its expenditure on that activity through a DSO is less than £100,000 a year.

Sources: Local Government Act 1988, s. 2 (2) and Schedule 1; The Local Government Act 1988 (Competition in Sports and Leisure Facilities) Order 1989 SI 1989/2488; The Local Government Act 1988 (Defined Activities) (Exemptions) (England) Order 1988 SI 1988/1372. Cm 1599 promises to extend CCT to the field of housing management as well as to further indirect services.

as to provide a clear definition and separation of the two roles and this approach was also endorsed by the main public sector accountancy body (Audit Commission 1989; CIPFA 1989: para 6.5 and see Figure 1). Once such an institutional separation of roles comes about, perceptions of interests and patterns of behaviour tend to change as a result.

If there is sufficient interest from the private sector to provide competition for DSOs, local authorities will inevitably come to be identified primarily with the client role, at any rate in relation to services subject to competitive tendering. After all, the client role will continue even if the DSO does not. Furthermore, the best a DSO can hope for is to beat the private sector at its own game and according to its rules. The client role, on the other hand, involves distinctively public, governmental functions:

- assessing consumer demand and satisfaction
- developing new ideas on service provision and quality
- defining desired levels and quality of provision
- planning for and securing adequate financial resources
- managing the competitive tendering process
- monitoring achievement against policy (Audit Commission 1989)

In practice, DSOs appear at present to be winning a substantial proportion of the work for which they bid (see e.g., Walsh 1991), but the Audit Commission's principal document on CCT is sceptical at a number of points about their long-term future (Audit Commission 1989). The view of central government is that:

> local authorities' role in the provision of services should be to assess the needs of their area, plan the provision of services and ensure the delivery of those services. There are also fields in which local authorities will continue to have important regulatory functions and providing roles. But councils should be looking to contract out work to whoever can deliver services most efficiently and effectively. (DoE 1991b: para 4.)

This formulation is nicely ambiguous, since it is not clear whether 'contract out' is being used in a sense which implies that the contractor is necessarily private. However, it remains the case that although CCT necessarily gives primacy to the client role in defining the purpose of a local authority in relation to those services which are subject to competition, it is not inconsistent with its retaining a continuing contractor role.

Figure 1
The Audit Commission's view of options for the client-contractor split:

	Unacceptable	Undesirable	Possible	Ideal
Members	Same Committee	Same Committee	Same Committee plus DSO + client sub-committees	Client Committee DSO Board
Officers	Same officers	Different officers in same departments	Client department DSO	Stand alone or umbrella DSO. Client departments plus perhaps contract supervision unit.

Source: Audit Commission (1989) p.6

As with the NHS internal market, CCT may benefit consumers of local authority services, but it does not give them legally enforceable rights to services, still less make them sovereign. The customer/client/purchaser is the local authority itself. Its authoritative decisions determine the supply of services. The 1988 Act creates a general duty not to take into account 'non-commercial considerations' in exercising certain contractual functions. This prevents local authorities from seeking to achieve most of the policy objectives which could be pursued through 'contract compliance'. Subject to this limitation, however, and within the ambit of their statutory powers and duties, exactly what services they buy with their money is for local authorities themselves to determine. CCT does not even require them to explore the comparative costs of different service levels (Hartley 1990).

Next Steps Agencies
Contracts in the NHS and competitive tendering for local authority services are directed towards separating the client (or purchaser) and contractor (or provider) functions. The broader aim is to effect a cultural change in the management of public services. The 'Next Steps' programme has been called 'the most ambitious attempt at Civil Ser-

vice reform in the twentieth century' (Treasury and Civil Service Committee 1990). It also involves a separation of the functions of deciding what a service should be and delivering that service cost-effectively. Again, the overall aim is to effect a profound cultural change, in order to improve the management of public services.

The desirability of cultural change in the civil service is a long-standing theme. The Fulton Report (Cmnd 3638) in the late 1960s emphasised the importance of specialist skills, as opposed to the civil service 'cult of the generalist'. It made recommendations to improve efficiency and effectiveness by the creation of accountable management structures with a clear allocation of personal responsibility. The Fulton Committee was favourably impressed by the Swedish model of small central departments making policy which was then executed by autonomous agencies. It recognized that this would raise Parliamentary and constitutional issues, but recommended early and further consideration of 'hiving-off' areas of civil service activity to autonomous public boards or corporations (Cmnd 3638: paras 188-191). No such examination was conducted in public, but 'hiving-off' took place through the creation of quangos such as the Manpower Services Commission and by putting the operation of bodies such as the Royal Mint and the Post Office on a more commercial basis.

Though the term is not used, 'hiving-off' is a central aspect of the 'Next Steps' programme, so called after the report of that name from the Prime Minister's Efficiency Unit (Efficiency Unit 1988). Again citing the Swedish model, the report recommended that executive functions of central government departments be transferred to agencies. These should have operational independence and responsibility, within a framework of policy, resources and performance targets set by departments. The central civil service should eventually consist only of a small core, engaged in the function of servicing ministers responsible for policy matters. However, the report did not address other features of the Swedish agency model. In particular it neglected to mention that Swedish ministers are by law prevented from interfering in matters which are the responsibility of agencies. Furthermore, Sweden not only has a developed system of administrative courts but also four ombudsmen, who carry out inspections on their own initiative as well as receiving complaints from citizens. The Swedish ombudsmen are also prosecutors and part of the authority their office enjoys stems from the fact that the Swedish penal code makes wilful or negligent maladministration a criminal offence (Ragnemalm 1991).

Following acceptance of the Efficiency Unit's recommendations, the first Next Steps agency was established in mid-1988. The pace of change thereafter has been rapid. By May 1991 more than fifty agencies had been established, covering over 180,000 civil servants (see Table 2). The largest is the Benefits Agency which has carried out many of the functions of the Department of Social Security since April 1991.

The Next Steps programme is not merely the implementation of Fulton after two decades. In the interim, a major change had occurred in perceptions of the weaknesses of the traditional civil service. The core problem was identified as the exclusive focus on policy-making as its *raison d'être* (Efficiency Unit 1988). Other tasks were regarded as of lower status and, in particular, the effective management of resources was neglected, particularly as a result of the lack of external pressures demanding improvement in performance. Rather than Fulton's prescription of more experts in a variety of specialisms, the aim of Next Steps is to improve the quality and efficiency of government through better management.

This aspect of Next Steps builds on the Financial Management Initiative (FMI), which in turn was the successor to Sir Derek Rayner's efficiency scrutinies of the early 1980s (see Harden and Lewis 1986: 134 and references). A major goal of both the efficiency scrutinies and the FMI was the control and reduction of public expenditure. However, the FMI also focussed on accountability for the effective management of resources, requiring 'a clear view of ... objectives; and means to assess, and wherever possible measure, outputs or performances in relation to those objectives' (Cmnd 9058). To this end, it sought to match responsibility for operational decisions with authority for committing resources and to delegate decision-making as far down the line as possible.

Next Steps goes further by separating the managerial or executive role of the agencies from the policy-making role focussed on ministers. In addition, each agency is headed by a chief executive who has responsibility for and autonomy in the management of the resources provided to it. The intention is that Next Steps should lead to a federal structure of more autonomous units (Cm 841). Ministers and departments should to the greatest extent practicable stand back and leave agency managers free to manage (Efficiency Unit 1991: 30).

Such independence is necessary to raise the status of management in the civil service, so that being an agency chief executive, for example, is seen as a worthwhile and high-status role for a high-flying civil servant. However, separation of agencies from departments is not just

Table 2
Next Steps Agencies Established by May 1991

	No. of Employees
Building Research Establishment	690
Cadw (Welsh Historic Monuments)	220
Central Office of Information[1]	730
Central Veterinary Laboratory	580
Chemical and Biolological Defence Establishment	580
Civil Service College	210
Companies House	1,150
Defence Research Agency	11,700
Directorate General of Defence Accounts[2]	2,100
Driver and Vehicle Licensing Agency	5.450
Driving Standards Agency	2,050
Employment Service	5,600
Forensic Science Service	580
Historic Royal Palaces	300
Historic Scotland	580
HMSO[1]	3,300
Hydrographic Office[2]	880
Insolvency Service	1,450
Intervention Board	910
Laboratory of the Government Chemist	320
Land Registry	10,400
Meteorological Office	2,250
Military Survey[2]	850
National Engineering Laboratory	430
National Physical Laboratory	820
National Weights and Measures Laboratory	50
Natural Resources Institute	390
National Health Service Estates	120
Occupational Health Service	100
Ordnance Survey	2,500
Patent Office	1,150
Queen Elizabeth II Conference Centre	70
Radiocommunications Agency	500
RAF Maintenance[2]	5,700
Rate Collection Agency (Northern Ireland)	280
Recruitment and Assessment Services Agency	320
Registers of Scotland	1,100
Royal Mint[1]	1,050
Scottish Fisheries Protection Agency	230
Service Children's Schools (North West Europe)[2]	2,300
Social Security Benefits Agency	68,000
Social Security Contributions Agency	6,600
Social Security Information Technology Services Agency	3,350
Social Security Resettlement Agency	510
Training and Employment Agency (Northern Ireland)	1,700
UK Passport Agency	1,200
	cont.

Vehicle Certification Agency	70
Vehicle Inspectorate[1]	1,650
Veterinary Medicines Directorate	70
Warren Spring Laboratory	320
	183,460
Customs & Excise[3](30 Executive Units)	26,800
Total employees	**210,260**

[1] Trading Funds
[2] Defence Support Agency. Figure does not include service personnel.
[3] Moving towards full operation on Next Steps lines following publication of Framework Documents.

Source: Goldsworthy 1991: 40

about raising the profile of management skills in the public service, it is also intended to put those skills to work. For agencies to be able to function autonomously, it is essential to be explicit about the objectives of a particular agency, the resources which it will have, the specific targets it is to meet and how its performance will be monitored. Government has accepted that the emphasis in setting targets should be on outputs rather than inputs (T&CSC 1990, Cm 1263).

Framework Documents

The key mechanism through which the above principles are put into effect is the 'framework document' (FD) for each agency. The original Next Steps proposal envisaged setting out the policy, the budget, specific targets and the results to be achieved; specifying how politically sensitive issues were to be dealt with and the extent of the delegated authority of management (Efficiency Unit 1988: para 20). No formal definition of a FD has ever been produced but the concept and its perceived importance have developed in the course of implementation of the programme. The Project Manager in charge of Next Steps (Sir Peter Kemp) has emphasised that each FD is a unique document, tailored to the requirements of the particular agency. However, although there is no standard pattern, there are certain common elements. A FD usually:

- sets out the status, aims and objectives of the agency and its services;
- makes clear the relationship between the department and the agency and in particular the rights and responsibilities of the

agency chief executive, with specific reference to financial planning and control and to pay and personnel matters;
- sets out, or provides for, the performance targets which the agency must achieve (and the possibility of alteration to performance targets in-year);
- provides for accounts and reports to be published;
- provides for regular review of the agency's performance by the department and for a major review of the FD itself after three years;
- provides for approval of a long-term corporate plan and/or an annual business or operational plan for the agency and for the role of these documents in relation to the above matters.

FDs are fundamental to the relationship between agencies and departments, but the precise nature of that relationship has not been clearly defined. The White Paper on financing and accountability of the agencies refers to the 'department as "owner" and where appropriate customer of the Agency' (Cm 914: para 2.7). The official history of Next Steps says its aim is 'to establish a more contractual relationship between the Chief Executive and the Minister' and speaks of the 'underlying principle of a "bargain"' between them (Goldsworthy 1991: 7). The Treasury and Civil Service Committee recommended that each FD should 'be regarded as a contract' (T&CSC 1988). In evidence to the Treasury and Civil Service Committee, Sir Peter Kemp described the minister and chief executive as being in 'a quasi-contractual position, though I do not particularly like that expression' (T&CSC 1990: Q 170). The description was nonetheless accepted by the Committee and quoted by the Efficiency Unit (1991: para 2.6).

Although emphasising that FDs are not legal contracts for the provision of services, but statements about how services will be delivered, government has accepted that ministers and departments should avoid intervening in matters delegated to an agency. Where intervention is judged, exceptionally, to be necessary outside the terms of the FD, or of the normal planning and resource allocation arrangements, then it should be done explicitly (Cm 841, Cm 1263).

The precise legal status of FDs will be considered in Chapter 5. However, it is clearly the intention that they should be a binding (albeit revisable) agreement of the respective rights and responsibilities of agency and department. Furthermore, they are meant to separate (i) responsibility for deciding what services an agency should perform and what targets it should meet, from; (ii) responsibility for the agencies' performance in delivering those services and meeting those targets. In other words, there is a split between departments and agencies like that between a local authority and its DSOs, or between a DHA and an NHS provider. FDs thus perform a function which is as 'contractual' as that of the other types of arrangement examined in this chapter. Next Steps is part of the more general move towards 'management by contract' in the public sector (Kemp 1990).

Chapter 4

The Dynamics of the Contractual Approach

The examples considered in the previous chapter illustrate the two defining features of the contractual approach to public services; (i) responsibility for deciding what service there shall be is separated from responsibility for delivering that service; and (ii) the division takes the form of an agreed definition of rights and duties, which is intended to be binding. This chapter will first distinguish the contractual approach, thus defined, from various party political goals. It will then argue that the approach works by creating a structural bias in favour of two constitutionally valuable developments: the reduction of unnecessary administrative discretion and the delegation of decision-making authority to accountable and effective units. However, if the contractual approach is to produce the latter result, the separation of functions must correspond to a genuine organizational independence. In turn, this can exist only if there is an appropriate legal and constitutional framework.

There is no necessary link between contract and (i) competition between different providers and/or different purchasers of service; (ii) expenditure reduction; (iii) contracting out the delivery of public services to private firms; or (iv) privatisation. However, neither the practice nor the rhetoric of contracts for public services has maintained a clear distinction between the contractual approach and these other elements. As regards (ii), in making public expenditure decisions government frequently acts on the basis of assumed efficiency gains resulting from competitive tendering or contracting out. Competitive tendering and CCT also link contract to (i) and (iii). Furthermore, some of the identifiable cost savings resulting from competitive tendering come from reduced labour costs; i.e. wage-cutting, redundancies, or both.

A legacy of the 1980s is the conceptual imprecision of the term 'privatisation'. It is often used in a way which ignores the distinction between contracting out the delivery of a public service and complete privatisation, in the sense that the provision of a service becomes purely a matter for market relations between private actors. Where competitive tendering leads to contracting out, privatisation may result, in the sense of sales to the private contractor of public assets formerly used by the in-house supplier. Alternatively, such privatisation of assets may come first, in the form of a management buy-out, or other sale to the private sector of a service provider as a going concern. Neither involves privatisation in the sense that the service concerned is no longer public.

In practice, the introduction of contracts for public services has involved all the above elements, in various combinations. Nonetheless, it is possible to isolate the intended purpose of the contractual approach *per se*. This is to ensure that there is a definition, both quantitative and qualitative, of what the service concerned is supposed to be and that there is a search to provide the service as efficiently and effectively as possible. It is important to recognise that the idea of improved management involves both elements and that the first - the specification of objectives - has constitutional value. If government is to be made accountable for its policy decisions then an essential prerequisite is that the policies must be publicly known. Furthermore, specifying objectives for marketable public services is a necessary (though not a sufficient) condition for establishing individual legal rights.

Improved management requires cultural change in the public bodies concerned towards greater effectiveness in identifying priorities, planning and monitoring outputs, and controlling input costs. Contract is both an element of and a stimulus towards such change, whether the service provider be private or public. How is it supposed to work? To answer this question it is necessary to examine the types of provision a contract may contain and the kinds of relationship which it can be used to create.

Two Types of Contract

Contract enables the parties to create a new legal relationship or to alter an existing one. This power can be used in two ways. Firstly, the parties may provide for specific mutual obligations; for example, that A shall paint the windows of x houses and that B shall pay £y for this service. Secondly, they may establish rules to govern their relationship, perhaps conferring authority to make further rules or discretionary decisions. Examples can be seen in the rules of clubs, or of other unincorporated associations, which are a contract between the members. Such rules may also provide for the resolution of disputes. Arbitration clauses are familiar in commercial contracts and the jurisdiction of a 'domestic tribunal' over members of a private organization has a contractual basis. In contrast to the first 'primary' type of contract, this 'secondary' [1] type is, in effect, a private constitution.

Every long-term relationship has a constitutional dimension. That is to say, it needs some method, accepted by the parties as legitimate, for establishing goals, resolving disputes and altering the ground-rules of the relationship itself. This need not always take the explicit form of a secondary contract. The general law of contract provides a flexible and highly liberal constitutional framework by default. Rights and duties under a primary contract can readily be altered by the mutual consent of the parties. This 'default constitution' also applies to a secondary contract. Its rules can be amended, or dispensed with, by the consent of the parties. Of course, neither the explicit provisions of a secondary contract nor the default constitution will necessarily capture all the assumptions, customs or practices which play a part in the relationship between the parties.

Any particular contract may contain both primary and secondary elements. The appropriateness of the balance between the two depends on its purpose and subject-matter. If there is a task to be performed which can be specified in sufficient detail for the purposes of the purchaser and if eventualities which may alter its requirements can be foreseen, then a primary contract is appropriate. This is also the case if the parties are content to accept the risk that changes in circumstances may alter the value or cost of their obligations. If neither is the case, then it may be more appropriate to rely in part at least on secondary provisions. Two rather different examples of such contracts are variation of price clauses as a way of sharing risks between the parties (Turpin 1989: 168) and framework arrangements, under which quantities of goods are called down as and when needed by the user.

Power-conferring Contracts

The framework agreement is an example of a particular kind of secondary contractual provision. It confers on one of the parties a discretionary power to specify the primary obligations of the other. For ease of reference, this type of contract will here be referred to as 'power-conferring'. Whenever the eventual performance envisaged by a secondary contract consists of obligations of the primary type, then there must be some way of ascertaining what the obligations are. They could be specified by a third party, or made dependent on conditions which are not controllable by either party. Otherwise, the contract must necessarily be - explicitly or implicitly - power-conferring.

In a commercial setting, it can rarely be sensible for one party to enter a contract in which the nature and value of the obligations to be performed is under the discretionary control of the other. A power-conferring contract only makes commercial sense in a limited range of circumstances and where the discretionary power is restricted in its scope and purpose so that it cannot be abused. More generally, whenever there are two parties whose interests are not identical, there is a danger that broad discretion under a power-conferring contract may be abused by the party which is entitled to specify the obligations, so harming the interests of the other.

Relationships between bodies with separate interests thus contain a built-in incentive towards avoiding the costs of a power-conferring contract. Instead, they will be more inclined to accept the risks of a primary contract, or if that is not possible, to restrict and confine as far as possible the power-conferring element of a secondary contract. The same considerations of rational self-interest also point towards primary contracts of a particular type. Rather than specifying the duties in terms of how an activity is to be carried out, they will focus on the outcome to be achieved. Otherwise, the party defining the obligations must itself do the work involved in relating the processes it prescribes to the desired outcome, rather than leaving this task to the other party. Since it is actually doing the job, the latter is better placed to make such decisions and to seize opportunities that may arise to make savings by achieving the desired outcome using more efficient processes. For these reasons, it makes sense for both parties if the primary obligations are specified in terms of outcomes rather than processes, so far as possible.

Rule-making, Accountability and Delegation

The use of contracts for public services thus creates a structural bias in favour of styles of management which have long been advocated by critics of traditional public administration. There is pressure to avoid unnecessary discretion and, where discretion is essential, to confine and structure it to avoid abuse. In effect, contract is both an incentive to rule-making and a way of making rules (cf Davis 1971). There is also pressure towards reliance on 'performance' rather than 'process' accountability (Smith and Hague 1971) and hence towards delegation of decision-making authority. In the NHS, for example, the provider/purchaser split involves significant primary elements in the contracts, although the move from 'process' (block contracts, constructed in terms of inputs) to 'performance' (cost and volume contracts, specifying outputs) will happen more slowly. Next steps framework documents have a large secondary element, establishing a private constitution for the relationship between the agency and the department. However, they also contain and/or provide for the establishment of primary obligations, specified so far as possible in terms of output/performance.

It would be a mistake, however, to think that the contractual approach to public services offers nothing new; that it is just another way of expressing certain principles of public sector organization which have been advocated for at least two decades. The new element is not 'consumer sovereignty', however, nor greater rights for individuals. Rather, it is the fact that the parties to the contract have separate interests. In this sense 'competition' is inherent in the contractual approach; not competition between different purchasers, or different providers of services, but in the contractual relationship itself. The public interest - i.e. the overall functioning of the public service in question - is not the responsibility of a single unitary organization, but instead emerges from the process of agreement between separate organizations, none of which has responsibility for the public interest as a whole.

It is this which is essential to the creation of a structural bias towards minimizing discretion and a focus on performance/outputs rather than process/inputs. The separation of interests provides the vital incentive to move away from an administrative structure which is the functional equivalent of an (incoherent) power-conferring contract, giving broad discretionary power to the provider to specify the primary obligations, subject to sporadic and *ad hoc* recall of that power by the 'purchaser'. Contract thus appears as a way of dissolving the old dilemma of 'independence versus control' (Smith and Hague 1971) by using the former to promote accountability.

Contract and the Separation of Interests

Although the separation of interests is vital to the contractual approach, many contracts for public services involve relationships in
which, although at 'arm's length' for some purposes, the parties have a
long-term commitment to each other. A district health authority cannot exercise a right of 'exit' by taking all its business away from a major
local hospital. The Secretary of State for Social Services cannot choose
between different Benefits Agencies to carry out this part of the
department's work. If there is any rationale for local authority DSOs
to exist at all, there must be a mutual commitment by contractor and
client to the authority, beyond the terms of a specific contract price
and specification.

Close relationships between government and private contractors
are nothing new. They are familiar, for example, in the field of defence
procurement. Furthermore, drawing on practice in the private sector,
the Treasury has encouraged government departments generally to
cultivate long-term relationships with suppliers. As Turpin puts it:

> The aims and principles of government procurement
> require a middle way between a detached, imper-
> sonal conduct of business and an almost symbiotic
> relationship (Turpin 1989: 70-71).

If a long-term relationship is mutually beneficial, then the parties have
an interest in maintaining it which goes beyond the short-term gains
which each makes, or could make, from the other. A 'middle way' needs
to recognize such interests and to deal with actual and potential
disputes so as to avoid conflicts that may destroy the trust necessary
for the relationship to continue. These same issues may arise in relations between public bodies with separate functions and interests.
Walsh, for example, points to the emergence of antagonistic and
conflictual client/contractor relationships in some local authorities as
a result of CCT (Walsh 1991: 84). On the other hand, also to be avoided
are various forms of collusion at the expense of third parties that may
occur between supposedly competing interests. It has been suggested,
for example, that private orderings may emerge between NHS purchasers and providers, subverting the intended effects of the contract
system (Hughes 1990). In the case of a public service, the 'middle way'
is even more complex, since the interests of the parties cannot be
defined solely in terms of even long-term mutual benefit.   Public
services are meant to serve the interests of citizens, customers and
consumers.

Regulation of the contractual process so as to preserve the 'middle way' raises the 'dilemma of accountability' again in a different form. It risks subverting the contractual basis of the relationship between the parties and hence the extent to which the contract represents the outcome of negotiation between genuinely separate interests. This is connected with a more general problem about the organizational separation of interests within the public sector.

Private Constitutions and the Public Constitution

It is possible to create organizations with a degree of functional independence ('quangos', as they used to be called) in a number of ways. There might seem to be no reason why a 'private constitution' embodied in a secondary contract should not itself perform the separation between different organizations, as well as providing for the relationship between them. One chief executive of a Next Steps agency in fact described the Framework Document in terms of a 'bill of rights' for the agency (T&CSC 1990: para 15). However, the explicit secondary dimension of a contract is always revisable on the basis of the 'default' constitution; i.e. through simple mutual consent of the parties. In the case of central government, this leads back not to arm's-length bargaining between private parties, but to the general public law constitution, characterized by ministerial responsibility.

As numerous commentators have remarked (e.g., T&CSC 1988), Next Steps is not the first attempt to restrict ministers to a strategic role in which they do not interfere in management decisions. The nationalized industries were also meant to have managerial freedom to make commercial judgements within a strategic framework. Ministers had statutory powers to issue formal directions to the industries' boards. Instead, they relied on so-called 'lunchtime directives', subverting the managerial independence of the boards on an informal *ad hoc* basis, for a variety of purposes and without accepting public responsibility for so doing. This involved a legislative rather than a contractual framework, but there is nothing in the concept of contract to prevent such a thing happening. On the contrary, whatever the private constitution established by a secondary contract, the parties can always agree to ignore it.

To exclude this possibility, a contract would need also to have a public constitutional dimension. In the case of a primary contract, this might be achieved by turning the obligations of the service provider under the contract into legally enforceable entitlements of individuals. This would not be possible for all primary contracts, but it could be achieved for some. In the case of a secondary contract, however, this approach could not be used. The problem is altogether more complex. To create a public constitutional dimension for a secondary contract between public sector bodies means confining and structuring ministerial responsibility and finding a new basis for legitimate authority in the space thus created.

Conclusion

The further one departs from the model of a discrete exchange between private actors, the more abstract the notion of contract becomes and the more work has to be done to construct a framework capable of delivering the intended results in a specific context. Contract offers no ready-made mechanism for organizing public services. However, the contractual approach does offer the possibility of greater accountability for public services, by specifying objectives and by delegating functions to accountable organizations with separate interests. It could also provide the basis for expanding individual legal entitlements by specifying the obligations of the service provider.

Long-term contractual relationships necessarily involve a private constitution, which may be explicitly constructed by a secondary contract, or the 'default' constitution provided by the general law in the case of a primary contract. This needs to be designed, and dealings between the parties within it managed, so as to avoid either destructive conflict, or cosy arrangements at the expense of outsiders. At the same time, regulation must not subvert organizational independence. To ensure such independence a public constitutional dimension is necessary. How far the existing legal and constitutional framework of contracts for public services is capable of providing this dimension is the subject of the following chapter.

Chapter 5

The Legal Framework of Contracts for Public Services

English common law has no concept of the 'public' or 'administrative' contract. Some special legal rules do apply to the contracts of public bodies; for example, a contract may not fetter the exercise of public powers. However, there is only one law of contract as far as the courts are concerned. The Crown has the same common law capacity to make a contract as a private individual. The power of local authorities to make contracts is subject to the *ultra vires* principle; unless the authority has statutory power to make a particular contract it is void. This is also true of other public bodies which derive their contractual capacity from statute.

Public bodies, like private organizations, make use of freedom of contract to deal on standard terms and conditions. Those applicable to central government contracts include provisions designed to protect the public interest (such as the 'break clause' permitting government to terminate the contract at any time, subject to indemnifying the contractor). Such clauses serve the same function as principles of law developed in jurisdictions which have a separate law of public contracts (Turpin 1989: 105-111).

There are public law principles which courts could develop to structure the discretionary powers conferred by freedom of contract on public bodies. Natural justice, for example, has been held applicable to the removal of a contractor from a local authority's approved list

(*R v Enfield LBC ex parte T. F. Unwin (Royden) Ltd, The Times*, 16 February 1989). Restrictions as to purposes or procedures could also be imposed on the exercise of 'secondary' contractual powers; for example, in relation to withholding payments or terminating a contract for unsatisfactory work. However, the principles of judicial review have not been regularly applied to the exercise of contractual functions by public bodies. Both the absence of any specific public law of contracts and the lack of judicial review of contractual functions can be traced to the constitutional theory, propounded by Dicey in the nineteenth century, that the rule of law is to be maintained through subjecting government to ordinary private law (Arrowsmith 1988, 1990).

The private law of contract is a complex body of sometimes conflicting rules and principles. Only a few basic aspects are mentioned here, which are of importance later in the chapter. A contract must be between at least two parties, each of which possesses contractual capacity. In the case of organizations, contractual capacity is connected with the more general concept of 'legal personality'. An organization has legal personality if it is the bearer of legal rights and duties, separate from those of its members, or of other organizations. A second key principle is 'privity'. In general, a contract creates rights and duties only for the parties. If A is in breach of a contract with B, C cannot bring proceedings against A. Only B is entitled to sue. Finally, there is the requirement of 'consideration'. That is, a contract must be a reciprocal transaction between the parties, involving mutual benefit and detriment. A mere promise is not a contract.

The Law of Contract and Consumers of Public Services
It can be seen from the above that not every bargain or exchange counts as a legal contract. One area which is somewhat obscure is the application of the law of contract to public services which are marketed. The courts decided in the eighteenth century that the Postmaster-General did not enter into any contract for the delivery of post. This decision has been followed in the twentieth century (*Whitfield v Lord Le Despencer* (1778) 2 Comp. 754; *Triefus and Co. v Post Office* [1957] 2 QB 252). Nineteenth-century judges analysed the statutory duties of companies supplying gas and electricity in the same way as those of public authorities providing sewerage or street-cleaning services. In both cases, the matter was discussed largely in terms of whether an action lay in tort for breach of statutory duty. That is, individuals could sue only if the statute imposing the duty had been intended to create private rights for their benefit. Since statutes rarely deal with the issue expressly, the question was usually one for judicial decision.

Such claims were often rejected on the ground that alternative means of enforcement were available, such as ministerial default powers or statutory penalties. In relation to public services generally, including those which are not marketed, this principle remains of great significance. Individuals only possess a legal entitlement to a public service if the courts hold that the statute creating a duty to provide the service was intended to create private rights. This they have been reluctant to do (see, as regards refuse, education and health services; *R v Kensington LBC ex parte Birdwood* (1976) LGR 424, Harris 1990, Longley 1990: 540-542). If the statute is held not to create private rights, individuals are restricted to public law remedies and even these may be excluded by, for example, ministerial default powers. [2]

The argument that the relationship involved in supplying and consuming gas should be analysed in terms of contract was specifically rejected in *Clegg, Parkinson and Co. v Earby Gas Co* [1896] 1 QB 592. The result was the same as that achieved by allowing the private railway companies (which did contract with their passengers) to rely on broad exclusions of liability for breach of contract. The different legal framework made little practical difference. Consumers had to take or leave the service levels offered by the provider and themselves bear the losses caused by service failures.

The most recent authority is *Willmore and Willmore (Trading as Lissenden Poultry) v South Eastern Electricity Board* [1957] 2 Lloyd's List Law Reports 375 (Adams and Brownsword 1987: 184). The relationship between the Board and the consumer was held not to be contractual. When the Board supplied electricity it was acting pursuant to its statutory duty to supply a consumer who demands such a supply, not fulfilling a contractual obligation. Courts have made a similar analysis of the supply of water by a local authority to a ratepayer (*Read v Croydon Corporation* [1938] 4 All ER 631) and of the payment of a prescription charge by an NHS patient (*Pfizer Corporation v Ministry of Health* [1965] AC 512).

Privatisation of the utilities has done nothing *per se* to alter the situation. This is hardly surprising since, as the nineteenth-century judges clearly perceived, the status of the supplier of public services as a private company or a public authority makes no difference to the basis of its relationship with its customers. The privatised gas, water and electricity industries remain under a statutory duty to supply (Gas Act 1986 ss. 9, 10; Water Industry Act 1991, ss. 37, 52-4; Electricity Act 1989, s. 16). Specific statutory provisions govern the setting of tariffs and impose a duty on consumers to pay. The Water Industry Act gives consumers an express statutory right to bring an action in respect of loss or damage caused by (in effect) negligent breach of the duty to supply water for domestic purposes (s. 54). If the reasoning in *Willmore* is correct, it would thus seem unlikely that ordinary 'tariff customers' have any contractual relationship with British Gas, a water undertaker, or an electricity supply company.

The Gas Act 1986 makes specific provision for a contractual relationship with non-domestic users in cases where the construction or enlargement of a main, or other works, are needed. A public gas supplier may refuse a supply unless the person requesting it 'enters into a written contract' containing various provisions (s. 10 (7)). The legislation for both gas and electricity also provides for 'special agreements' between the supplier and consumers of large amounts of gas or electricity (Gas Act 1986 s. 14 (4); Electricity Act 1989 s 22).

The Gas Act says nothing further about such agreements and their status is unclear. In *Clegg, Parkinson and Co v Earby Gas Co* there was no express agreement, merely the conduct of the parties in supplying and using gas. In other cases in the nineteenth and early twentieth centuries, contracts were held to exist between utilities and customers where special express agreements were made. The judge in the *Willmore* case would have been prepared to find a collateral contract in these circumstances, although the actual supply would have remained the performance of a statutory duty. Although the issue does not appear ever to have been raised in relation to the utilities, it may be doubted whether the performance of a statutory duty could be sufficient 'consideration'. However, courts now seem ready in some circumstances to hold that performance of an existing duty can be sufficient consideration to support a contract (Adams and Brownsword 1990).

Under the Electricity Act, the 'rights and liabilities of the parties to a special agreement shall be those arising under the agreement'. Disputes under a special agreement may be referred to the Director General of Electricity Supply by either party. The effect of these provisions appears to be that even if a 'special agreement' regarding electricity supply is a contract (which remains uncertain), the ordinary courts would have jurisdiction only if both parties so wished.

The Water Industry Act contains a duty (subject to exceptions) to provide new non-domestic water supplies, but provides for 'terms and conditions' to be determined by agreement or, in default of agreement, by the Director-General of Water Services according to what appears to him to be reasonable (s. 56). However, unlike the Electricity Act, the Water Industry Act does not provide for the Director to determine disputes under an agreement and the duty under s. 56 is not one to which the exclusive enforcement powers of the Secretary of State or Director applies. Nor is there any specific provision for breach of the statutory duty to be actionable by non-domestic consumers. There would thus seem to be a strong case for regarding agreements under s. 56 as contracts and this may be the intended effect of the obscurely worded s. 55 (7).

When it was responsible for both postal and telecommunications services, the Post Office enjoyed a statutory exemption from any kind of liability through court proceedings. This provision was generally understood as applying to tortious liability, because of the long-standing principle (discussed above) that there was no contract involved. It was repealed in 1981 when postal and telecommunications functions were separated, but the assumption appears to have been that the contractual immunity established by the courts survived. The 1969 Act gives the Post Office power to establish schemes of charges and conditions for the services it offers and allows it to recover a charge 'in any court of competent jurisdiction *as if* it were a simple contract debt' (s. 28 (5), emphasis added). Section 30 provides for liability in respect of lost or damaged postal packets, the amount of such liability being determined, or regulated, by a s. 28 scheme.

The Telecommunications Act 1984 imposes no statutory duty to supply. Section 8 of the statute provides for an equivalent duty to be imposed as a condition of a licence to operate a telecommunications service and this power has been exercised (see BT's licence Schedule 1, Part 2 condition 1). However, BT's conditions for telephone service describe themselves expressly as the terms and conditions of a contract with the customer.

It can be seen from the above examples that the law of contract often does not apply when the provider of a public service is carrying out a public legal duty. This is so even in the circumstances - which superficially look highly contractual - of a consumer paying for a marketed public service. Exceptions to this principle are of uncertain scope. Furthermore, the legal framework which does govern the legal entitlements of individuals to public services is a patchwork, composed of accidents of history and legislation and of discretionary judicial decision-making about the tort of breach of statutory duty. Turning now to relationships between public purchasers of services and providers, we find again that, for one reason or another, contract does not provide a general legal framework. The areas considered in Chapter 3 above will be examined in turn.

Contracts in the NHS

The contracts which link purchaser and providers in the reformed NHS fall legally into three distinct categories (see Figure 2). Some are ordinary private law contracts: i.e. when a district health authority (DHA) or fund holding GP practice contracts with a private provider, or when a private purchaser contracts with an NHS provider. The arrangements by which a DHA 'purchases' services from its own DMUs are 'structured as contracts', but 'enforced through ordinary management processes' (Department of Health 1989: para 2.1). NHSME has stressed the importance of a clear separation of functions within districts, in effect requiring 'Chinese walls' to be set up within authorities (Longley 1990: 547). The separation of functions has no legal dimension, however. It is impossible for there to be a private law contract between a DHA and its own DMUs because the latter have no legal personality separate from that of the authority itself.

Figure 2

Contracts for Health Services

Provider

		PRIVATE	NHS TRUST	DMU
Purchaser	DHA	Ordinary Law	NHS Contract	Management / NHS Contract
	FUND-HOLDING G.P.	Ordinary Law	NHS Contract	NHS Contract
	PRIVATE	Ordinary Law	Ordinary Law	Ordinary Law

Contracts within the NHS where there is no direct management relationship fall within a new statutory category - the 'NHS contract'. This is defined by section 4 (1) of the 1990 Act as:

> an arrangement under which one health service body
> ("the acquirer") arranges for the provision to it by
> another health service body ("the provider") of goods
> or services which it reasonably requires for the pur-
> poses of its functions.

An NHS contract is not subject to the ordinary private law of contract since the Act provides that 'it shall not for any purpose be regarded as giving rise to contractual rights or liabilities'. Instead, either party may refer a dispute to the Secretary of State for determination. The latter may decide the matter himself, or appoint another person to do so. The principles which should be applied in resolving disputes under an existing NHS contract are not laid down in the Act or Regulations. However, guidance from NHSME states a (qualified) principle of freedom of contract: 'the presumption in determining a dispute is likely to be that the outcome will give effect to the agreement which was originally reached, rather than a new agreement which the parties should have reached' (NHSME 1991: para 9).

The same guidance emphasises that the formal procedures are intended to be a last resort and that every endeavour should be made to resolve disputes locally. All NHS contracts should include clauses for agreed 'arbitration' if a party believes that a contract has been broken and the arbitrator, usually the Regional General Manager (RGM), should be specified in the contract. In the case of a pre-contractual dispute, both parties are expected to seek assistance from the RGM, or RGMs if the parties are from different Regions, in order to obtain an impartial view of reasonable terms for the proposed contract.

Local Authority Services

If a local authority obtains services from a private supplier, whether as a result of compulsory competitive tendering or not, it does so through an ordinary private law contract. Agreements under the Local Authorities (Goods and Services) Act 1970, under which one local authority supplies services to another, also take effect as contracts in private law. However, if a local authority decides after complying with the CCT provisions, that a 'contract' should be awarded to its own direct service organization (DSO) there is usually no private law contract. The reason is that the DSO is unlikely to have legal personality separate from that of the authority itself.

It is possible for a local authority to set up companies which have separate legal personality, but this is not a requirement of the CCT legislation. Nor does the legislation itself constitute DSOs as separate legal persons. Instead, special accounting requirements are imposed on authorities. As was seen in Chapter 3 above, the effect of the accounting requirements is to bring about an organizational separation between 'contractor' and 'client' functions within the management structure of the authority. However, this separation is not given any external legal form and any contracts into which the DSO wishes to enter are made in the name of the authority.

Next Steps Agencies

Drawing attention to the experience of ministerial intervention in the nationalized industries, the Treasury and Civil Service Committee (1988) recommended that:

> Each framework agreement, which sets out what is within the authority of the Chief Executive should be regarded as a contract. The Minister would then be entitled to overrule the Chief Executive, but only by way of a formal note...

The Committee was given an explanation, dressed in the language of high constitutional principle, of why this was legally impossible. Contracts made by government departments are made in the name of the Secretary of State, who acts on behalf of the Crown. Since an agency is not legally separate from the department, its contracts are also in law contracts of the Crown and the Crown cannot contract with itself. Whilst this analysis is constitutionally impeccable, much of it is also redundant. Framework documents cannot be private law contracts because agencies do not have legal personality separate from that of the body their contract would be with. However, there would have been no constitutional obstacle to Next Steps agencies having separate legal personality if government had chosen to give the programme a legislative basis and to make agencies statutory corporations, without Crown status.

The Legal Framework of 'Private Constitutions'

The fact that the private law of contract has only a limited range of application to 'contracts' between a public body and a service provider would matter little if, within its range of application, it provided an appropriate legal framework for primary and secondary contracts and if, in areas where it does not apply, other legal principles provided such a framework. Neither is the case. Individual legal rights under primary contracts and organizational independence in the public sector will be examined in turn.

Individual Rights

Legal entitlements of individuals to public services are important, both in themselves and as a supply-side incentive to effective service provision under primary contracts. However, where there is an ordinary private law contract between a public body and a service provider, the doctrine of privity prevents individuals from acquiring any rights under the contract in relation to the services. If there is no such contract, then usually the arrangement lacks any specific legal status. In this sense it is true that, for example, Next Steps framework documents are 'not legal documents' (Goldsworthy 1991: 26). The NHS contract, on the other hand, is defined under the 1990 legislation. In effect, it is a special form of 'public law contract' (Longley 1990). However, the statutory framework for dispute resolution gives individuals no standing to complain about breach of an NHS contract.

Even though they are neither contracts, nor possess any other formal legal status, statements published by public bodies may generate 'legitimate expectations' and so create rights which are enforceable by individuals in the courts as a matter of public law. Government has accepted that a framework document should normally be published and that if it is kept secret, in whole or in part, the relevant minister should be expected to justify the decision (Cm 524: 9). The NHSME has said that 'contracts for health services, with both public and private providers should be publicly available once they are signed' (NHSME 1990b: 4.14). This statement appears to include all three categories of 'contract', including those between DHAs and their DMUs. Under the CCT legislation, detailed specifications of the work to be carried out have to be published.

Publication creates the possibility of legitimate expectations, but this is not yet a well-developed area of law. The scope of the doctrine is uncertain, as is the extent to which it can give rise to substantive rather than procedural rights. In the past, courts have sometimes refused to give public law remedies in respect of contractual relationships (e.g. *R v IBA ex parte Rank Organization*, *The Times*, 14 March 1986). It is possible that they may exclude the principle of legitimate expectations precisely because it would infringe the doctrine of privity. Even if there are legitimate expectations, it is by no means clear that public law remedies would lie against a private contractor, though again there is a line of authority which could be expanded to achieve this result (*R v Panel on Takeovers and Mergers, ex parte Datafin* [1987] QB 815).

To sum up, the possibility exists that individuals could, through public law, acquire enforceable legal rights as a result of contracts between a public body and a service provider. However, the law in this area is uncertain. The courts might respond to the accidents of litigation by developing the doctrine of legitimate expectations into a 'citizens' charter' for public services provided through contract. On the whole, this must be considered unlikely.

Organizational Independence in the Public Sector
Relationships between Next Steps agencies and departments, DHAs and DMUs and local authorities and their DSOs cannot take the form of private law contracts, because the parties have no separate legal identity. Legal identity precedes and cannot be derived from a contractual relationship. Thus if an organizational separation of interests in the public sector is to have any legal dimension, it must come from public law. Next Steps agencies, local authority DSOs and health service DMUs have no corporate personality deriving from public law; otherwise they would be able to make contracts. This same lack of legal identity also means that they could not bring proceedings for judicial review.

Whilst accepting that framework documents could not be contracts, the Treasury and Civil Service Committee recommended that ministers should adopt a 'self-denying ordinance' in respect of matters delegated to the agencies under FDs. This has been accepted by government (T&CSC 1990: para 19, Cm 1263) and parliamentary questions relating to operational matters are in fact being referred by ministers to agency chief executives. However, the only way in which the self-denying ordinance could acquire a binding quality would be as a 'constitutional convention'. The generally accepted theory of conventions tends simply to legitimize whatever happens. If conventions were understood as legitimate constitutional expectations (Harden 1991) there would seem to be good reason for regarding the 'self-denying ordinance' as a convention; or rather as a modification of the convention of ministerial responsibility. However, this is almost certainly a minority view at present.

Even if the self-denying ordinance were a convention its effect would simply be to give some binding quality to the words of a framework document. The fact that this would, in itself, be revolutionary should not blind us to its limitations. If disputes arise as to the meaning of a FD, or as to how it should be interpreted in unforeseen circumstances, constitutional convention provides no mechanism for independent dispute-resolution. Nor do FDs themselves create any such mechanism.

The NHS
In contrast with Next Steps agencies, NHS Trusts are statutory corporations. They are established by order made by the Secretary of State, who also appoints the chair of the board of directors. Each Trust owns the land, building and equipment with which it operates and has an originating capital debt equal to the value of these assets.   They have

a duty to meet financial objectives set by the Secretary of State and a rate of return of six per cent must be earned on the current value of assets.

A Trust has power to do anything which appears to it to be necessary or expedient for discharging its functions, including the power to acquire and dispose of land and other property, borrow money, enter into both NHS contracts and ordinary contracts and employ staff on such terms as it thinks fit. Trusts are also specifically empowered to engage in research and to treat private patients. They also enjoy the powers to raise extra revenue conferred on the Secretary of State by s. 7 (2) of the Health and Medicines Act 1988. The latter include powers to manufacture and supply goods, deal in land, supply services, develop and exploit ideas and intellectual property and charge on a commercial basis for what they do in the exercise of these powers.

The managerial independence of an NHS Trust is thus based on a clear legal separation of its interests from those of the other organizations to which it relates. However, as we have seen, its contracts with other NHS bodies are of a special public law kind. Disputes about them go not to the courts, but to the Secretary of State. The latter's dispute-resolution powers extend to the pre-contractual bargaining stage for NHS contracts. If one party claims that the other is abusing an inequality of bargaining power between them, the Secretary of State can, in effect, write a contract and impose it on the parties. This departs radically from the ordinary law of contract. Once negotiations for an NHS contract have begun, it is not possible for a party to withdraw without the permission either of the other party, or of the Secretary of State. Furthermore, the principle of equality of bargaining power has been invoked in the ordinary law of contract mainly in the context of consumer transactions, rather than in those between corporate bodies.

The National Health Service Contracts (Dispute Resolution) Regulations (1991 SI 1991/725) govern cases in which the Secretary of State appoints an adjudicator to decide a dispute. An adjudicator has discretion whether or not to adopt an exclusively written procedure and may also consult persons whose expertise he considers will assist him in his consideration of the matter. However, natural justice must be observed. Each party is entitled to make representations, to see and comment on representations made by the other side and to make observations on the results of any consultation. The adjudicator's determination must be recorded in writing and accompanied by reasons.

The Regulations do not apply unless determination of a dispute is delegated to an adjudicator. Nor is there any legislative statement of principles to govern the determination of disputes about NHS contracts, save the implication that the pre-contractual powers may be used to remove the effects of inequality of bargaining power. If disputes were consistently referred to adjudicators, the requirement of reasons could encourage a clear set of principles to emerge, in which the role of the minister's policy framework would need to be clearly articulated. However, despite the fact that the dispute-resolution powers are judicially reviewable and that an NHS Trust would have standing to seek review, it is possible that no consistent principles will emerge. The arbitration role of Regional General Managers (probably not reviewable) and the discretion not to delegate formal disputes to an adjudicator could together lead to a managerial, rather than a quasi-judicial, approach to disputes.

This is more than just a theoretical possibility. The Secretary of State is not an independent arbiter in disputes between Health Service bodies. On the contrary, he remains legally and constitutionally responsible for ensuring the provision of health services under the 1977 Act. The key point here is not the independence of Trusts, but the role of DHAs. Although they have separate legal identity as statutory corporations, they remain agents of the Secretary of State and carry out their purchasing functions on his behalf. They do so without any clearly defined independent role. There is no equivalent of a framework document for DHAs and so in any dispute involving a DHA, the Secretary of State is potentially an interested party.

The structure of the NHS reforms thus provides no legal basis for a separation of interests between DHAs and DMUs. The basis does exist for such a separation between Trusts and DHAs; there are tantalising glimpses of a public law contractual framework with its own principles to regulate the relationship between them. However, there is no clear separation of functions between the DHA and the Secretary of State. This lack of a constitutional framework for the exercise of the purchasing function risks subverting its separation from the provider function.

DSOs and Local Authorities
In the circumstances of CCT, the separation of client and contractor interests could be (a) defined in terms of a right of private contractors to participate in a fair competition and (b) enforced through a mechanism for protecting that right. However, such a right is not contractual.

Quite the opposite; it derives from public law restrictions on the freedom of contract enjoyed by local authorities.

Like central government, local authorities can make use of freedom of contract both to decide with whom to contract and to establish the 'secondary' terms and conditions on which they are prepared to do business. For example, standard CCT contracts require 'performance bonds' to ensure that, if a private service provider fails to carry out a contract, the authority is able to recoup the costs of arranging for the service to be provided by other means.

If the separation of client and contractor functions in local authorities is to be effective, there must clearly be some mechanism to prevent local authorities from evading the disciplines of CCT by using their freedom of contract so as unfairly to disadvantage private suppliers. This is not a simple matter, even in relation to the award of contracts. The general principle applicable to public contracts is that the lowest bid should not automatically be accepted. Rather, the bid which represents the best overall value for money should be chosen (Treasury 1988, 1990: para 47). This involves complex issues of judgement as does, for example, the question of when a performance bond is excessive.

The 1988 Act does not directly provide for a right of private contractors to participate in fair competition under CCT. Its solution to the problem of regulating the separation of client and contractor interests in local authorities is to provide, as one of the conditions which must be fulfilled before a DSO may lawfully carry out work, that:

> the authority, in reaching the decision that they
> should carry out the work and in doing anything else
> ... in connection with the work before reaching the
> decision, did not act in a manner having the effect or
> intended or likely to have the effect of restricting,
> distorting or preventing competition (s. 7 (7)).

The Secretary of State has wide-ranging powers to obtain information from local authorities in respect of suspected breaches of this (and other) conditions and to give subsequent directions (ss 13, 14). These powers are expressed to be without prejudice to any other remedy available, but the extent of such remedies and their efficacy are both doubtful. The more straightforward course for an aggrieved contractor whose primary concern is to get the local authority to play fair rather than to get damages for its not having played fair in the past, is to complain to the Secretary of State.

In effect, the 1988 Act gives the Secretary of State primary jurisdiction over disputes about the award of contracts and about pre-contractual phases of the relationships of local authorities with their DSOs and with private service providers. This is a quasi-judicial function which must be exercised fairly *vis-à-vis* the local authority and there is no doubt that the Secretary of State's decisions are judicially reviewable (see *R v Secretary of State for the Environment ex parte Knowsley Metropolitan Borough Council, The Independent*, 29 September 1991). Advice on the interpretation of 'anti-competitive behaviour' has been given by circular and updated after experience of the first round of bidding (DoE 1991a).

The separation of interests between DSOs and local authorities is thus reinforced by an external dispute-resolution mechanism. Whether or not the Secretary of State is the ideal person for the role, there is no doubt that he is independent in the sense of not being constitutionally accountable for services to which disputes relate. Furthermore, although not explicitly created as a way of protecting private contractors, they can in practice set the mechanism in motion, though they have no specific legal right to do so, nor even to have their complaint heard. However, for so long as the Secretary of State's policy remains that there should be fair competition between DSOs and private contractors, the 'rights' of the latter define and ensure the continued separation of interests between local authority client and contractor roles.

Conclusion

Neither the private law of contract nor public law provides a coherent legal framework for individual rights in contracts for public services. Nor do they provide such a framework for the separation of interests in the public sector. As regards the former, there is a lack of clear principles and in some cases uncertainty even as to how an arrangement should be analyzed in legal terms. There is also a lack of clear principles to govern the relationship between separate interests in the public sector. Only in the context of competitive tendering involving the private sector can the latter problem be solved by using third party rights to fair competition as a proxy. Even here, however, there is continued dependence on the discretionary policy choices of ministers rather than legal rights.

Elsewhere, arrangements in the NHS go halfway towards creating a mechanism to generate principles to govern some of the contractual relations in the internal market. However, the mechanism can be bypassed if ministers so choose. As regards Next Steps agencies, the problem is to get to first base and give framework documents some binding quality. Even if this can be done, there is no public law basis for departmental/agency relations outside the terms of the FD itself. The absence of principles governing relationships between separate interests in the public sector is partly the cause and partly the effect of a lack of correspondence between intended function and legal form. Before considering in Chapter 7 the questions of quality and performance, it is worth considering how this dissonance between function and form may be affected by European Community law.

Chapter 6

European Community Law

Through a series of Directives, a European Community law of public procurement is being established. [3] 'Procurement' has, in this context, a broad meaning and includes procedures for the award of almost all public contracts (excluding defence). Directives concerning supplies and works contracts have been in force since the 1970s, but had little impact until they were amended and strengthened more recently. A significant measure is the 'compliance' Directive, to be implemented by December 1991. This requires national remedies to be available to persons with an interest in obtaining a particular contract, who are harmed by an infringement of the Directives, or of national implementing measures. The remedies available must include the suspension of contract awards, setting aside of unlawful decisions and damages.

In Britain, the works and supplies Directives were implemented by administrative guidance and instructions. In late 1991, two sets of regulations under the European Communities Act 1972 transposed them into domestic law (The Public Supply Contracts Regulations 1991 SI 1991/2679; The Public Works Contracts Regulations 1991 SI 1991/2680). These also implement the compliance Directive, in respect of contracts subject to the relevant Directive, by conferring jurisdiction on the High Court to give appropriate remedies. Extension of the Community legal framework to include public service contracts has now reached the stage of a formal proposal for a Directive (see box).

The Proposal for a Services Directive (COM (91) 322 Final)

The Community law of public contracts is complex and can only be sketched in the barest outline here. The drafting of the later Directives has aimed to produce an increasingly standard pattern and the services proposal follows closely the format of the works Directive. Key requirements are:

- contracts above a threshold value (200,000 ecu for most public service contracts) must usually be put out to competitive tender and advertised in the Official Journal of the EC. Bodies awarding contracts are free to choose between 'open' procedures (in which all interested contractors can present an offer) and 'restricted' procedures in which only invited contractors (of whom there must be at least three) may submit tenders. 'Negotiated' procedures, in which contracting authorities consult at least three service providers of their choice and negotiate the terms of the contract with one or several of them, may only be used in defined and limited circumstances.

- Examination of the suitability of tenderers and award of the contract are governed by rules about the criteria which authorities are permitted to use and evidence which they must accept, or are permitted to demand, as proof that certain criteria are fulfilled. There are only two bases on which contracts may be awarded: either lowest price only, or the 'most economically advantageous tender'. This must be decided in advance and made clear in the contract notice. If the 'most economically advantageous' basis is chosen, the contract notice must specify the criteria to be applied, where possible in descending order of importance.

- Public authorities must keep adequate records and give reasons for certain decisions. The services proposal requires a written report to be drawn up for each contract awarded. *Inter alia*, it must include names and addresses of all tenderers and the reasons why they were rejected or selected; and the name of the successful tenderer and the reasons for selecting the tender. Unsuccessful tenderers or candidates who so request are entitled to a statement of reasons for their rejection within 15 days.

The proposed services Directive would have an important direct impact on the law of public service contracts in Britain. Competition in contracted out services would be a general legal requirement rather than merely a policy backed up by law in specific contexts. The 'transparency' requirements for record-keeping and the giving of reasons would be a significant move towards open government. The more government policy puts emphasis on competitive tendering for public services the wider this range of effects will be.

There may also be indirect effects of equal importance. The proposal is written on the assumption that the contracts to which it relates will mainly be for *indirect* services. The only specific provision which it makes for *direct* services concerns 'public service concessions', in which the service provider receives 'the right to exploit the service or this right together with payment'. The Directive does not, however, present any obstacle to contracts for direct services in forms other than the concession. The Commission's commentary on its original proposal makes clear that the Directive is neutral as between in-house and market service provision and that it is not intended to apply to the former:

> The Directive in principle covers all situations in which the client and the service supplier are legally separate entities, and in which their relationship for the purpose of supply of services is of contractual nature (COM (90) 372, para 80).

This makes two assumptions about domestic law. First that it is possible to identify what counts as a contract and second that there is a clear correspondence between the functional independence of an organization and its legal status. As we have seen, neither assumption is correct in the British case. However, implementation of the existing public procurement Directives by Statutory Instrument may force greater clarity on the relationship between form and function in domestic law. The services Directive may have the same impact on the definition of a 'contract'.

The Range of Application of the Public Procurement Directives

The Directives apply to 'contracting authorities'; i.e. central, regional and local government and 'bodies governed by public law'. The latter term is defined as those bodies:

- established for the specific purpose of meeting needs in the general interest, not having an industrial or commercial character, *and*
- having legal personality, *and*

- financed, for the most part, by the State, or regional or local authorities, or other bodies governed by public law; or subject to management supervision by those bodies; or having an administrative, managerial or supervisory board, more than half of whose members are appointed by the State, regional or local authorities or by other bodies governed by public law.

None of the Directives makes specific provision for bodies which have budgetary independence, but no separate legal capacity to make contracts. The specific problem is in deciding when the thresholds for triggering the Directives' requirements have been reached. For this purpose, the Directives require 'aggregation' of a series of legally separate contracts entered into by a single contracting authority. The Treasury's view (Treasury 1988b) is that the Commission is understood to accept that independent procurements by separate parts of a purchasing authority can be treated in isolation for the purpose of applying the aggregation rules. The Statutory Instrument implementing the supplies Directive was drafted on this basis thus creating what is, in effect, a legal definition of budgetary devolution within the public sector. This occurs, according to the Statutory Instrument, where goods are procured 'for the sole purposes of a discrete operational unit within the organization of the contracting authority', to which the decision to procure goods of the type in question has been devolved and which makes the decision 'independently of any other part of the contracting authority'.

The question of whether an 'operational unit' makes independent procurement decisions thus becomes legally decisive. In the case of Next Steps agencies, this could mean that the interpretation of framework documents and the question of whether ministers have observed the 'self-denying ordinance' as regards procurement issues will have to be treated as justiciable matters. Although less constitutionally dramatic, the same applies to relations between DHAs and DMUs. Unit general managers are to be given delegated powers whenever possible to contract on behalf of the DHA in relation to their unit's business (NHSME 1990b: para 2.6).

The Proposed Services Directive and the Definition of a Contract

If the proposal for a services Directive comes to fruition in anything like its present form, it will be necessary to decide to which contracts it applies. Public service contracts are defined by the draft Directive as 'contracts for pecuniary interest concluded in writing between a service provider and a contracting authority'. This cannot be restricted to private law contracts, since to do so would exclude much of the procurement of services by public bodies in jurisdictions in which the concept of a public or administrative law contract exists. It seems clear that its provisions will apply when local authorities are required to advertise work under the CCT legislation, even though if a DSO is successful there is no contract. Presumably the authority will then be required to comply with the provisions of the Directive which relate to non-award of an advertised contract.

NHS contracts might also fall within the scope of the Directive. The 1990 Act says that they are contracts. Although not uncontested, the better view would seem to be that they are a special type of public law contract (Longley 1990, but see Jacob 1991). The statutory provision that NHS contracts 'shall not give rise to contractual rights or liabilities' merely means that - like contracts governed by *droit administratif* in France - such contracts are not justiciable by ordinary courts. District health authorities are 'bodies governed by public law'; they have separate legal personality, are financed by the state and could hardly be said to be of a 'commercial or industrial character'. It would thus seem *prima facie* that a DHA intending to purchase health services from an NHS Trust or from a DMU that is part of another health authority will have to comply with the Directive.

Although aimed at breaking down barriers to trade between member states, the major impact of the Directive would be likely to be on relations between UK public and private health care providers. Contracts with private health providers, governed by private law, clearly fall within the proposed Directive. The effect of bringing NHS contracts within its scope would be that private health providers in the UK could also bid for NHS contracts. Furthermore, any form of competition between Trusts and DMUs would raise the question of whether all DHAs' requirements for health services should be advertised, with the same solution being adopted if a DHA's own DMU wins as in the case of local authority DSOs.

It is conceivable that the special nature of the 'internal market' might justify excluding NHS contracts from the ambit of the Directive. They could then be regarded as a form of budgetary transfer within the public sector. However, to do this it would be necessary to abandon any idea of competition between public and private health providers to supply DHA requirements. If such competition existed, there would seem to be no good reason for allowing only UK private providers access to the DHA market. The effect of the proposed services Directive on the NHS may thus be to force government to make a definite choice; between either a genuine market, with competition between public and private sectors to provide services to DHAs, or a clear ring-fencing of the NHS as involving only public providers.

Quality

Article 29 of the proposed Directive provides that, if contracting authorities require quality certification of a service provider, this must be based on the relevant EN 29000 European standards series. It had earlier been proposed that the requirement of such certification should be mandatory and this may still happen in the longer term.

European standards are produced by the European Committee for Standardization (CEN) which comprises the national standardization organizations of the EC and EFTA member states. EN 29000 is identical to the UK national standard for quality systems, BS 5750, issued by the British Standards Institution (BSI). Producers may use BS 5750 to check their own 'quality' systems. Purchasers may require compliance with the standard and operate their own checks. Third-party certification, of the type envisaged by Article 29, can be given by BSI or commercial organizations accredited by the Secretary of State for Trade and Industry, who acts on the advice of the National Accreditation Council for Certification Bodies.

'Quality', both as noun and adjective, has become a familiar term in recent discussion of public services in Britain. The next chapter will examine what 'quality' means in the EN 29000/BS 5750 sense and how this and other concepts of 'quality' relate to accountability for public services and to the legal entitlements of individuals.

Chapter 7

Quality and Performance

.

'Quality' seems to have become as much of a public sector buzz-word as 'efficiency' was a few years ago. As a slogan, 'efficiency' gains much of its power from ambiguity between a number of quite precise meanings (see Birkinshaw *et al* 1990: Chapter 5). 'Quality', in contrast, is a rather vague term. It was argued in Chapter 4 above that contracts for public services tend to promote the 'confining' (reducing the scope) and 'structuring' (controlling the manner of exercise) of discretionary power (Davis 1971).

Aspects of this confining and structuring have had the 'quality' label attached to them. The potential value of these developments in terms both of individual legal rights and accountability will be examined in this chapter. 'Quality' also has a less benign aspect. Conceptual confusion about the term risks obscuring the continued existence of discretionary power both in the supply of and, more crucially, the demand for public services. 'Quality', it will be argued, is not a substitute for consumer sovereignty. Ways of making such continued discretionary power accountable must be sought elsewhere.

Supply Side Aspects of Quality

At the end of the last chapter, the possibility was mentioned of quality certification of a service provider under BS 5750. BS 5750 was originally developed to apply to manufacturing processes. It consists of guidelines for management systems to ensure reliability in meeting a

customer's specification or performance requirements. It needs interpretation and application in specific contexts; something which is often
part of the role of consultants accredited to certify that the standard is
met. To qualify, an organisation must show that it can identify customers' needs effectively and then meet them reliably. BSI describes
the standard as providing 'a formalized check-list of requirements for
a company's quality system' and as being 'simply common sense set
down on paper in an organized way' (BSI Quality Assurance, undated).

The concept of 'total quality management' (TQM) is associated
with the BS 5750 approach, but goes beyond it to embrace broader
questions of management style and philosophy which are not
susceptible to formal certification processes. It is identified with
Japanese industrial success, based on controlling costs whilst satisfying
customers (Department of Trade and Industry 1990). 'Quality' in both
the BS 5750 and TQM senses is based on orientation towards customer
satisfaction.

Over the past few years there has been considerable interest in the
application of BS 5750 and TQM to public services (see e.g.,
Department of Employment 1990). Some local authorities have
obtained BS 5750 certification for particular DSOs and have required
it from contractors under CCT. The Citizen's Charter proposes the
introduction of a 'Chartermark' for public services which meet what
will be a published 'Charter Standard', though the precise relationship
of this to BS 5750 is not clear.

BS 5750 does not specify quality on the 'demand' side by defining
the particular standard or level of service that should be provided. It
simply requires that the provider be able to identify a defined standard
which meets the customer's requirements and have management
systems capable of ensuring that the service is delivered to that
standard. The principles of quality assurance that underlie BS 5750
were originally developed by purchasers such as the Ministry of
Defence and Marks and Spencers to ensure that goods supplied to
them would consistently meet their specifications. Promoted now as a
way of helping suppliers be successful in a competitive market, BS 5750
is premised on the idea that ultimately the customer has power over
the standard and level of service demanded. 'Quality' in the BS 5750
sense is thus a 'supply-side' concept. It is not in itself a mechanism for
demand-side empowerment of the consumers of a public service.

'Service contracts'

As we have seen, the use of contracts for public services has similar
'supply-side' objectives. The separation of purchaser/provider func-

tions forces a definition of what is being purchased, preferably in 'output' terms. The provider is encouraged to be effective because it is accountable for performance of the contract. However, although the 'customer' is a public body, not the individual consumer, the contractual obligations of the provider can be expressed as performance levels which the consumer has a right (in some sense) to enjoy. Local authorities have taken the lead in pioneering such 'service level agreements', or 'service contracts' (see now Association of Metropolitan Authorities 1991).

These can also be used even if there is no provider/purchaser split. One of the principles of the proposed 'Charter Standard' is publication both of the standards of service that a customer can reasonably expect, and of actual performance achieved against those standards (Cm 1599: 6). This should not be understood as a kind of second best compensation for the absence of a right of exit. Services are 'public' because public authority has decided that they should exist. Citizens are entitled *qua* citizen to know what the service is supposed to be and what performance has been achieved. They are also entitled *qua* citizen not to be dependent on the exercise of unnecessary discretionary power.

Public Service Compensation

Publication of service standards is in itself a powerful mechanism for structuring discretion. It requires the question of what standard is appropriate to be addressed expressly. Failure to meet the promised standard provides a legitimate basis for criticism and complaint. However, to create individual rights analogous to those enjoyed under a contract, there must be a means for individuals to enforce performance of the service, or obtain damages. The idea of combining the publication of standards with 'public service compensation' for failure to meet them has been put forward as part of the Citizen's Charter debate (Consumers' Association 1991; Pirie 1991). This is an old idea with a new name. A statute of 1710, for example (9 Anne c 10, s. 22) required post-horses to be provided within half an hour of a request to do so. In the event of failure, a penalty of £5 was imposed, to be divided equally between the Crown and the complainant.

Public service compensation schemes already exist in relation to most of the utilities. The Electricity Act 1989 gives the Director General of Electricity Supply power, subject to the Secretary of State's approval, to make regulations prescribing performance standards and levels of compensation for tariff customers (s. 39 and see The Electricity (Standards of Performance) Regulations 1991, SI

1991/1344). Disputes may be referred to the Director by either party. The Water Industry Act 1991 gives similar powers to the Secretary of State to make regulations on the basis of proposals submitted by the Director General of Water Services (ss. 38-39 and see The Water Supply and Sewerage Services (Customer Service Standards) Regulations 1989 (SI 1989/1147 as amended by SI 1989/1383).

A similar scheme of performance standards and compensation exists for British Telecom, but with no direct statutory basis. Instead it has been incorporated into BT's contractual conditions for telephone services (OFTEL 1989). A compensation scheme for gas has also been negotiated between the regulator (OFGAS) and the industry, to be introduced from April 1992. However, the legal status of the scheme is unclear, since it is not statutory and there appears to be no contract between gas suppliers and tariff customers. The main focus of public demand for compensation has been British Rail, whose standard conditions exclude liability for non-performance (although there is an *ex gratia* compensation scheme).

In view of the fact that BR's relationship with its customers is contractual, it might seem ironic that the National Consumer Council should argue that the 'Citizen's Charter should establish a relationship between public services and the consumer which is as close as possible to an explicit contractual relationship involving enforceable rights' (NCC 1991: para 19). However, the 'contract' element of 'service contracts' should be understood not as referring to a specific legal category, nor as making comparisons with the 'guarantees' offered by suppliers of private services (such as dry-cleaners). Rather, it is a claim that individuals should not be dependent on the exercise of arbitrary discretionary power by those carrying out public functions. They should have clear entitlements and legal redress when they do not get what they are entitled to.

As we saw in Chapter 1, this commitment to the rule of law cannot be identified exclusively either with contract or with public law. However, to think of individual rights in relation to public services as a 'new contract' (Pirie 1991: 8) is no less appropriate a way to try to expand those rights than to think of state-conferred benefits as a 'new property' (Reich 1964). The confusion to be avoided is that of thinking that the 'new contract' has anything to do with consumer sovereignty over the demand for public services.

The Demand Side of Quality

'Quality' in the sense that there should actually be a standard for a service is a supply-side concept. 'Quality' is also used in a commendatory sense to refer to high standards. The decision as to what the standard for a service should actually be is part of the overall 'demand' for a service. In a competitive market for private services, 'quality' in this sense is a matter of consumer sovereignty, whereas standards for public services are a matter of authoritative decision. In the case of the utilities, the power to set standards is sometimes formally in the hands of the Secretary of State, sometimes of the regulator and sometimes is not a specific legal power at all.

The Citizen's Charter promises legislation to 'bring the formal powers of each regulator in this area up to the levels of the strongest', so that all regulators have adequate powers to set guaranteed service standards (Cm 1599: 45 and see now the Competition and Service (Utilities) Bill). Part of the job of the regulators is to promote efficiency by requiring high levels of service whilst squeezing prices. But as well as this 'supply-side' aspect, the power to set standards also potentially involves a decision to allow prices to rise to support higher service levels or *vice versa*. Furthermore, the interests of shareholders and of consumers as 'customers' of the utilities are clearly in competition. This demand side role of the regulators of utilities does not yet appear to have been fully recognized in public debate about their functions.

Other key 'demand' decisions concern the level of resources to be devoted to a particular service and the setting of priorities. (Of course, depending on how detailed and extensive the specification of standards is, it may have implications both for priorities and for overall cost). In the case of central government services financed largely out of general taxation, such as the NHS, overall resource levels are set by government through the mechanism of the Public Expenditure Survey (PES), for the results of which ministers are accountable to Parliament. Consumers and customers of marketable services which are cash-limited in this way are in competition with each other; all subsequent demand decisions involve an element of rationing. In the case of the utilities, on the other hand, 'rationing' is effected through the price mechanism.

Some of the Next Steps agencies are wholly or partly self-financing through charges. They can be taken outside Parliamentary Supply procedure by operating 'trading funds' (Trading Funds Act 1973, as amended by the Government Trading Act 1990). A trading fund makes it possible for levels of activity and expenditure to vary in line with receipts from charges, so that the volume of production can be responsive to market signals. However, the legal requirement of the Act is that a fund should be managed so that the revenue of the fund consists 'principally' of receipts in respect of goods or services provided (s. 4 (a) (1) (i)). The extent to which an agency is subject to market disciplines thus depends on whether it faces competition, what proportion of its normal revenue comes from receipts and on ministerial decisions through the PES process. Service priorities are a matter for agreement between an agency and the minister and should appear in the framework document, for which ministers are accountable to Parliament.

As regards health authorities, however, matters are less clear. Public debate has tended to focus on the role of NHS Trusts as providers of health care rather than on DHAs as purchasers. The former RAWP (Resource Allocation Working Party) formula for allocation of funds to health authorities has been discontinued and replaced by a formula based on population, weighted for age and morbidity. As we have seen, the Secretary of State remains statutorily responsible for the provision of health services. The NHS Management Executive, however, says that DHAs are 'responsible for using their resources to secure comprehensive, high quality and effective health services for their residents' (NHSME 1990b: para 2.3). Where precisely health care priorities are supposed to be set is not certain, particularly since the NHS Policy Board and Management Executive are non-statutory organizations. However, the requirement that DHAs publish their contracts with providers may eventually make transparent how much discretion has in practice been delegated to them.

Delegation of Demand Decisions Through Contract

Procuring public services through contract helps identify responsibility for 'demand' decisions. In principle, the split between provider and purchaser makes clear that it is the purchaser who sets the demand. However, as is shown by the example of DHAs, the precise location of demand decisions may remain uncertain in the event of confusion about the purchaser's independence of 'third parties'.

We saw in Chapter 4 that authority to specify the 'demand' for a service can be expressly allocated through a secondary, power-conferring contract. When the contract is a primary one, delegation of this power to the producer may occur *de facto*, without any express power-conferring provision. This happens unless the service to be provided is specified in output terms that are both concrete and complete. The task of writing such a specification is difficult and demanding, even for services which are relatively straightforward, like refuse collection and street cleaning. Detailed specifications for CCT contracts are often enormous documents.

Part of the significance of the contractual framework is that the separation of the interests of the parties provides an incentive to explore the limits of the possible in terms of specifying primary obligations. However, for more complex services, a detailed contractual specification of outputs in precise concrete terms may be impossible. Primary obligations have to be expressed as inputs, or in abstract output terms. For example, GPs' contracts with Family Health Service Authorities provide that 'a doctor shall render to his patients all necessary and appropriate personal medical services of the type usually provided by general practitioners' (quoted in Jacob 1991). The discretion which this kind of contractual provision confers *de facto* on the provider may be 'confined' by rules specifying more precise requirements for part of its range of application. This has been done with GP contracts (Jacob 1991: 257-9). Such discretion may also be 'structured' by the use of performance indicators.

Performance Indicators (PIs)
Considerable effort was made during the 1980s to develop PIs as a way of promoting the '3Es' of economy, efficiency and effectiveness. The defining feature of a PI is that it can be measured. Measuring performance in ways that are meaningful in terms of the objectives of public services is difficult both conceptually and practically, though there is real scope for the quantification of output and performance in government (Levitt and Joyce 1987). In the literature, a distinction is drawn between the use of PIs as 'tin-openers' or 'dials' (Carter 1991). Tin-openers are simply descriptive. They do not provide a norm against which performance is directly assessed. If there is a statistical norm, deviation from it is an invitation to investigate and probe to find out why. Dials are standards against which achievement can be assessed directly (such as the percentage of first-class letters arriving the next day). They can be used prescriptively to establish performance targets, although this is not inevitable.

When used prescriptively, PIs may directly specify objectives; i.e. things which are valued outcomes in themselves. In a contractual context these can be formulated as specific obligations, so confining rather than structuring discretion. For example, health service contracts specify times within which certain things should be done, e.g., for an accident and emergency service, all patients to be registered within five minutes of arrival (NHSME 1990b: 61). Work on developing such indicators may thus extend the area within which service standards can be adequately specified through primary contracts. The Citizen's Charter promises to use some such standards as 'service level agreements' with patients, by publishing guaranteed maximum waiting times for in-patient or day-care treatment for key waiting list treatments such as hip replacement (Cm 1599: 47).

Other PIs measure things which are not important *per se*, but serve as a proxy for an objective which is not susceptible to direct measurement. Quite frequently, PIs perform both functions at the same time. Financial indicators, for example, may be used to specify targets which are important in themselves (since economy is one of the '3Es') and which also serve as proxies for more abstract concepts such as management effectiveness. However, proxy PIs are vulnerable to a form of 'Goodhart's Law'. This states that any previously observed relationship between one variable and another disappears if one of the variables is targeted with a view to achieving a desired outcome for the other. Formulated in relation to monetary policy, its application to PIs can be illustrated by the use of citation indices as a PI for academic research quality. Insofar as citation is a proxy for the value of a piece of work this relationship is liable to be undermined by academics forming citation circles to boost one another's ratings (Cave *et al* 1988).

As applied to a PI, 'Goodhart's law' is really another way of saying that the decision as to whether it functions as a dial or a tin-opener is not always under the control of the person establishing it. In an administrative context, there can be room for managerial flexibility in the use, interpretation and status of PIs to try to compensate for this. In a contractual context, however, if a proxy PI is specified as a primary obligation the purchaser is bound by it, even if it turns out not to produce the results intended.

There are more satisfactory ways of using PIs to structure the discretion of the provider of a service under contract. Rather than using a PI prescriptively, the requirement can be to provide information. This can be used in assessing whether more abstract primary obligations have been met, or in further contractual negotiations. Secondary provisions can be used to require the provider to agree appropriate PIs with the purchaser, to develop PIs itself, or to co-operate in the development of PIs by others. Next Steps framework documents, for example, provide for specific indicators to be agreed annually with the department and included in operational or business plans. In the NHS, contracts require provision of information to monitor performance and participation in the development of 'medical audit' of the effectiveness of treatment.

'

'Quality PIs'

The term 'quality' has a number of meanings. There is the 'supply-side' sense of consistent adherence to a standard. There is the demand-side sense of 'high quality', which involves a judgment about the standard. What standard can reasonably be expected depends upon decisions about resource-allocation and priorities as well as on the producer's efficiency within a given resource level. 'Quality' is measurable in the first sense, where in effect it is a by-product of performing a basic task well (Carter 1991). However, actually to perform the task of measurement may be extremely complex and expensive, as in the case of medical audit.

'Quality' is not directly measurable in any other sense. 'Quality PIs' must necessarily relate to the first sense of the term, or be proxies, with the limitations already examined. This is really just another way of saying that it is not possible entirely to eliminate the *de facto* delegation to a service provider of power to determine the 'demand' for the service, except by a complete and concrete specification of primary obligations in terms of outputs. However, such discretion can be structured in the ways already examined.

Customers, Consumers and Quality

Complaints from consumers or customers of a service can play a number of overlapping roles. Numbers of complaints can be used as a 'tin-opener' PI, to guide other forms of monitoring, or as a 'dial'. In the latter role, they can be both a proxy for the quality of the service and an objective in their own right. For example, some local authority CCT contracts for refuse-collection and street-cleaning use numbers of complaints as a prescriptive PI to trigger penalties on the contractor, or to require remedial action. The complaints process clearly needs to be independent of the provider if 'Goodhart's Law' effects are to be avoided.

As we have seen, if there are published service standards, then individuals can be given enforceable rights to the standard of service prescribed. Complaints may then function not simply as a PI but as an avenue of redress. In this case, attention needs to be given to design of the complaints mechanism. In the case of service standards which are concrete, the central question of whether the standard has been met may often be very straightforward to resolve, without the need for particularly elaborate procedures. However, if the standard is prescribed only in general and abstract terms, giving the service provider a measure of discretion over exactly what the service is to be, complaints play a different role. The question of whether or not the standard has been met is a matter of judgement.

It is possible to use complaints in this circumstance simply as a PI, structuring the provider's discretion. However, they also provide an opportunity for 'checking' (Davis 1971) the exercise of discretion. This requires a more elaborate complaints mechanism, since it is necessary to examine and question the provider's judgement. Giving 'voice' in this way to consumers (and where services are rationed, to would-be consumers) can be an effective way of empowering them on the 'demand' side of quality in relation to services which cannot be entirely specified in concrete terms, such as, for example, education and social care.

Standard-setting

In addition to checking discretion on the demand side through individual complaints, there are opportunities to empower consumers and customers in relation to specifying demand through standard-setting. The Citizen's Charter sets out as a general principle that:

> The people affected by services should be consulted. Their views about the services they use should be sought regularly and systematically to inform decisions about what services should be provided (Cm 1599: 5).

One of the requirements for award of the 'Chartermark' will be evidence that the views of those who use a service have been taken into account in setting standards. One way of doing this is through market research. However, a PI which allows such research to be commissioned and paid for by the provider has obvious limitations. Organizations competing in a market have good reasons for designing surveys to discover what their customers actually want. Those not in a competitive environment may seek to design surveys to justify what they themselves want. Some independent element is necessary if PIs focussed on market research are to structure effectively the discretion of the provider in specifying demand.

More generally, an effective substitute for the democratic 'voice' of consumer sovereignty requires identification of all the decisions which establish the demand for a public service. As we have seen, this includes the allocation of resources and establishment of priorities; purchasing decisions by public bodies; standard-setting by purchasers, regulators, or by the provider; the establishment of PIs to monitor a service (including those which seek to measure customer satisfaction);

and the determination of complaints about services specified in abstract terms.

Furthermore, just as regulators have a mix of demand and supply-side functions, the same can be true of processes of inspection and audit. These can be used to check the exercise of discretion on the demand side, as well as to monitor the supply-side performance of concrete obligations. However, if inspectors are selected and paid for by the service provider the same problem arises as with market research. The absence of consumer sovereignty means that there is no incentive to use inspection as a way of improving performance. Inspection must be genuinely independent if it is to structure the provider's discretion.

The minimum goal that can be aimed at in terms of structuring such discretionary demand decisions is transparency. Beyond that, it is possible to substitute for the absence of consumer sovereignty by the participation in the making of demand decisions of representatives of consumer or customer interests; e.g., consumer councils for the utilities and Community Health Councils in the NHS (Longley 1992). This involves recognizing that, in relation to public services, enforceable individual 'contractual' entitlements cannot be a complete substitute for consumer sovereignty in specifying demand. If we are serious about the values of contract then such methods of participation should be seen as an essential aspect of subjecting the 'demand' for public services to control by the 'voice' of consumers, customers and citizens.

Chapter 8

Towards a Constitutional Framework for Public Services

Use of the language of contract implies a commitment to the expansion of the legal rights of individuals as consumers of public services. The 'new contract', like the 'new property' should be understood as a claim, based on the rule of law, not to be dependent on discretionary public power for the things necessary for individual autonomy. If taken seriously, it requires the state to do more, not less. Guaranteed legal rights to public services are not cheap and are unlikely to be paid for wholly by efficiency savings. Such rights can sharpen public perception of the link between standards of service and the resources available to the provider. It might, for example, be more difficult to reject the argument that additional money should be spent on the NHS, if the result of not doing so were quantifiable in terms of an increase in a legally guaranteed maximum waiting time for operations of various kinds.

Contract is not, however, a ready-made set of solutions to the problems of organizing public services. It cannot deliver consumer sovereignty through individual market choices. Familiar questions thus re-emerge in the contractual setting, although sometimes in an unfamiliar guise. The first of these, addressed in the previous chapter, is how to 'confine, structure and check' discretionary administrative power (Davis 1971). It matters little whether the challenge to the rule of law posed by the existence of such power be understood in terms of a delegation from a sovereign Parliament, or as a derogation from consumer sovereignty.

There are two traditional answers to the problem of discretionary administrative power (Stewart 1975). The first is the 'transmission belt' theory; administration merely implements the policies of ministers accountable to Parliament. The doctrine of ministerial responsibility applies to every level of policy-making; from the allocation of resources by PES, through the establishment of priorities, to the setting of service standards and their application to individual cases. There is supposed to be no arbitrary and unaccountable power, because for every discretionary administrative decision a minister is accountable to Parliament. Ministerial responsibility remains a major constitutional symbol. Ignoring the broader constitutional context of the Swedish agency model, government has promised that 'Next Steps will involve no diminution in Ministerial accountability to Parliament' (Cm 914: 16). This is true, but only because ministerial accountability to Parliament has always been largely a 'dignified' element of the constitution (to use Bagehot's term) concealing the fact of unaccountable discretionary power (Harden and Lewis 1986).

The other traditional basis for justifying the exercise of discretion is expertise. Whether the neutral elite of unassuming experts be scientists, social scientists, doctors or managers, questions of judgement about what ought to be done tend to get swallowed up by technical questions about how things can be done. Most public services involve not a single 'customer' or 'consumer' interest, but overlapping and often competing interests of citizens, consumers and a variety of customers. An undue emphasis on management using its expertise to promote 'customer satisfaction' carries the risk that fundamental questions about the purpose of a service will receive *sub rosa* answers for which no one is accountable. An associated danger is that the purchaser/provider split will lead not to a clear separation of functions and interests *between* organizations, but rather to a split *within* organizations between managers and those actually providing the service (Jacob 1991: 257).

Insofar as there is a genuine separation between providers and purchasers, the problem of discretion appears again in the form of the 'quango' (in its popular sense of a quasi-autonomous public sector body). How are the purposes of such bodies defined, who controls them and to whom are they accountable? If the answer remains 'to Parliament *via* ministers', the independence of the body concerned is subject to gradual erosion or sudden collapse. A tendency towards over-monitoring of Next Steps agencies has already been identified (Efficiency Unit 1991: 3.15, 3.19; Price Waterhouse 1991), echoing similar problems in the relationship between Departments and an earlier generation of quangos, such as the Housing Corporation (Lewis and Harden 1982). On the other hand, if quangos exercise discretionary powers which are not subject to ministerial intervention how can this be constitutionally legitimate, except on the inadequate basis of 'expertise'?

Although contract is not a panacea for the problems of discretion, it does offer an opportunity to make real progress towards greater accountability by clearly identifying who is responsible for a policy, what it is, whether it is being carried out in practice and if not, why not. The purchaser/provider split promotes delegation to accountable provider units, although the independence of the purchaser may sometimes be less clear. However, on the demand side, the contractual relationship at least requires there to be a clear view of the purpose of the contract and thus a consistent set of policy objectives. It also requires a specification of what the provider is supposed to do or, at any rate, some effective way of making the provider accountable for its contractual performance.

The contractual framework inevitably leaves some unstructured, unchecked discretion, but the appropriate basis for comparison in terms of the aspirations of the rule of law is with the realities, not the theory, of ministerial responsibility. 'Customer satisfaction' is a simplistic notion which, if pushed too far, risks being a cloak for arbitrariness. However, to a large extent ministerial responsibility itself operates as precisely such a cloak.

Contract and Political Choice

Just as political intentions are not a substitute for a constitutional and legal framework for government action, so it is a mistake to identify such a framework with the particular purposes that happen to be pursued through it. Using a phrase that has become well-known, Peter Hennessey referred to concern that the Next Steps project should be a piece of 'transferable technology', as valuable to a future Labour as to a Conservative government (T&CSC 1990: 60). More generally, the separation of purchaser and provider functions has no party political implications. 'Contract' in this sense has no necessary connection with privatisation, contracting out, or competition between different providers and/or purchasers.

Even CCT, which does necessarily involve competition and the possibility of contracting out the delivery of public services to the private sector, can be disentangled from other parts of government's political strategy towards local authorities. For example, the CCT provisions are separate from the prohibition on the pursuit of non-commercial policy objectives through contract. The requirements of the European Community law of public procurement are simply that such policies be transparent and do not discriminate against firms from other member states (*Gebroeders Beentjes BV v The State (Netherlands)*, Case 31/87 [1990] 1 CMLR 287). A government that so wished could give local authorities and other public bodies a power, or even a duty, to pursue non-commercial objectives through contract.

Competitive tendering and contracting out have also been associated with cutting wages. Again, this is not inevitable. A government which thought fit to do so could restore the 'fair wages resolution' as a form of contract compliance, legislate for a minimum wage or, for example, give local authorities power to pay their employees such wages as they thought fit within the CCT framework and adjust cost calculations in awarding contracts accordingly. The desirability or otherwise of all or any of these things is not the issue. They could all be done within an organizational separation of purchaser and provider and even within the context of competitive tendering.

A New Legal Framework?

The legal framework of public services is complex and inadequate, both as regards individual rights and in relation to contracts between providers and purchasers within the public sector. The 'Citizen's Charter' addresses primarily the first of these issues. It sets out a number of principles that will underlie the 'Charter Standard' including, as we have seen, publication of the standard of service that the customer can reasonably expect and also well-signposted avenues of complaint, with independent review where possible (Cm 1599: 6).

The chosen route for implementation of these principles is the 'Chartermark', which providers of public services will be able to apply to use in a way analogous to certification to BS 5750. At the time of writing, a number of things remain to be clarified; including the process by which criteria for the Chartermark will be developed and who will decide whether or not it should be awarded. Quality certification of private services operates as a convenience to the purchaser and a market asset to the provider. It is a product of consumer sovereignty, not an alternative to it. In relation to public services there needs to be some substitute for the 'voice' of consumer sovereignty as a way of ensuring that consumer interests are properly taken into account in the design and operation of a certification system.

Those awarding the Chartermark need to be clearly identified and publicly accountable. Adoption and amendment of Charter Standard criteria should be the subject of 'notice and comment' rule-making proceedings. That is, proposed criteria should be published, public comment invited and the final criteria be accompanied by a statement responding to cogent comment (Harden and Lewis 1986: 235-7). There should also be the possibility of hearings before the award of the Chartermark, particularly if this is contested on the ground, for example, that published service standards are not sufficiently precise, or that they neglect the interests of certain customers or consumers.

If the Charter Standard is to do an effective job of defining principles and procedures for empowering individuals *vis-a-vis* the providers of public services, its development will need to be a complex process. We have seen, for example, that there are a number of functions which complaints mechanisms can serve. In particular they can be a way of enforcing concrete published standards, or of empowering individuals when such standards are stated in abstract terms. The Citizen's Charter deals with enforcement in terms of 'public service compensation'. This is a short cut, both as regards liability and quantum, although there are still issues to be resolved about how it can most satisfactorily be administered. However, not all attempts by individuals to enforce concrete standards, or to obtain compensation for loss caused by their breach, can be dealt with in this way; particularly where a standard is abstract. If these matters are not to be left to the chances of litigation about 'legitimate expectations', some clear principles need to be developed about the function and purpose of complaints mechanisms.

Furthermore, there are many different forms of complaints mechanism available. In the past decade or so, for example, a bewildering variety of 'ombudsman' schemes has appeared in the private sector, seeking to capitalize on the international success of the public sector ombudsman idea. Cm 1599 also raises the interesting possibility of using lay adjudicators for dispute resolution in some circumstances. Part of the job of devising a public sector standard for complaints mechanisms must be to establish principles about what sorts of system are appropriate in different circumstances, about how they should work and about what further remedies should be available if a grievance remains unresolved. In sum, development of the Charter Standard ought to be regarded as a major legal undertaking, comparable in its scope and importance to the establishment of principles governing administrative tribunals and inquiries, following the Franks Report of 1957 (Cmnd 218).

Purchaser/provider Contracts

The Citizen's Charter describes Next Steps framework principles as 'semi-' rather than 'quasi-' contractual; perhaps because 'quasi-contract' has a specific (and unrelated) legal meaning, perhaps in recognition of the fact that 'quasi-' is almost always a signal that the concept it qualifies is inadequate (as in, e.g., quasi-judicial and quango). The legal framework for purchaser-provider contracts, examined in Chapter 5, is indeed inadequate. Only the ordinary law of contract is generally available as a way of giving legal validity to such agreements. Those which do not, or cannot, fit into this category have no clear legal status at all.

Contracts between the provider of a public service and a public body which purchases it on behalf of citizens, customers and consumers should always be published. They specify what the public service is and are appropriately to be compared with delegated legislation. Assurances have been given about the publication of contracts in the NHS and of Next Steps framework documents (but not business or operational plans, which may contain specific performance targets). However, there is no legal duty to publish. Citizens, customers and consumers are dependent on the exercise of discretionary administrative powers. Nor do the assurances specify when or how contracts should be published. It is important to establish the general principle that all purchaser-provider contracts should be published rather than decisions being made *ad hoc*.

Publication of purchaser-provider contracts is the bare minimum in terms of structuring the discretion of those whose decisions constitute the 'demand' for public services. Since citizens are unable themselves to decide what to buy with the money that purchases direct public services, they are entitled both to monitor how such decisions are made on their behalf and to be assured that a 'hard look' has been taken at what is being purchased and why. If 'consumer sovereignty' is to be more than an empty slogan, then what is needed is a judicially-monitored public law procedural framework to surround sites of demand decisions, including requirements such as 'notice-and-comment' for the establishment of service priorities, identification of customers and setting of performance standards.

In effect, this means creating a procedural alternative to ministerial responsibility and expertise as the basis for the legitimacy of public sector organizations making demand decisions; a surrogate for democratic voice through consumer sovereignty in the market. Such requirements might also help to prevent the possibility of 'contractual capture' in which a purchaser's decisions are unduly influenced by the interests of the provider. Naturally, there are limits to the extent to which the pre-contractual process can be opened up in this way. Not all contracts are significant enough to merit this treatment and there are also genuine issues of commercial confidence when there is competitive tendering.

A 'Public Law Contract'

Despite its flexibility in permitting the parties to agree whatever 'secondary' contractual provisions they wish, the law of contract cannot be used to constitute a public sector organization as a legally independent body. The parties to a contract must already have separate legal identities. Even if this problem did not exist, the 'default constitution' provided by the law of contract can always be used by the parties to revise whatever private constitution they have agreed. In the public sector this leads back, not to bargaining between independent organizations, but to the great hydra of the British constitution; ministerial responsibility. To have legal validity, organizational independence in the public sector must originate in public law. Functionally, such independence can only be maintained by public law.

A revised form of NHS contract, in which the role of the minister's policy in the dispute-resolution process was clearly structured (as in, e.g., land-use planning appeals) could provide a model for a general public law contract, potentially applicable wherever the functions of purchaser and provider of a public service are split. Such a public law contract, with its own principles governing formation, pricing and dispute-resolution, is appropriate to a particular kind of independence for public sector organizations. That is one in which express secondary contractual provisions are dependent for their interpretation and application on shared values and purposes that go beyond those of - even long-term - commercial self-interest.

Guidance from the NHS Management Executive states that 'establishing an NHS contract should not be approached as a legalistic or adversarial exercise but as the opportunity to discuss and agree how improvements to patient care can be secured...' (NHSME 1990b: i). However, 'legalism' in the sense of the term used by the NHSME merely reflects the commercial context from which specimen contracts were drawn (ibid: 126). The real problem which the NHS contract needs to address is how to define the relationship between organizations which have separate interests, other than in purely commercial terms. At one level, this involves ideas like a duty to bargain in good faith - both in the pre-contractual phase and in re-negotiation during the course of the contract - which are not part of the ordinary law of contract. Even more fundamentally, it means that all aspects of the contractual process, including dispute-resolution, need to be conducted against the background of a shared 'public service mission', defined in terms of the purposes of the service concerned.

A public law contract in this sense is clearly not compatible with competitive tendering. Whether it is compatible with 'managed' competition between different providers in an 'internal market' may be tested in the NHS. As far as contracting out without competition is concerned, there is no reason why the concept of a public law contract should not be defined so as to permit it to exist between a public purchaser and certain kinds of private body.

Given that the purpose of a public law contract would be to allow for secondary provisions to be interpreted according to shared values and purposes, to enter such a contract with a commercial firm would be self-defeating. Voluntary or non-profit organizations may have the appropriate organizational value structure although if, in the future, contracts for public services fall within the scope of the EC public procurement regime, it may be necessary to structure such 'contracts' as conditional grants. The ordinary law of contract could continue to be used for contracting out services which can be specified solely in terms of primary obligations, or with secondary provisions that can be satisfactorily interpreted and applied in a commercial context.

It would not be necessary, or possible, for there to be a detailed definition of each 'public service mission', nor for there to be fixed rules prescribing when a public law contract should be used. The availability of such a contractual regime would require the purchaser actually to address the question of whether the 'public service mission' made an ordinary private law contract with a commercial provider inappropriate. This would have two important consequences. Firstly, it would be necessary to identify different categories of 'private' service provider. At present, no clear distinction is drawn in discussions of contracting-out between commercial firms which seek to make profits, non-profit organizations and voluntary bodies which rely on unpaid labour. Secondly, it would be necessary for the purchaser to focus on the question of why a service is public in the first place.

A public service is one which exists not because of choices in the market, but because of a public decision that it should exist. This decision cannot be understood exclusively in terms of political choice, subject to accountability through voting in a political market. Partly it is a matter of economic rationality in identifying 'spillover' effects or externalities; benefits and burdens which the market ignores. It is also a matter of individual rights. The concept of the rule of law is a seamless web of form, procedure and substance. The concern that individuals should not - like the clients (customers? consumers?) of the Social Fund - be dependent on unnecessary administrative discretion, is part of a more general commitment to the autonomy of the individual which underlies contract and the rule of law.

In order for the individual to be a market actor in a modern society, able to make contracts that express individual choices, certain things are essential. As regards these essentials, the formal right of the individual not to enter a contract is of almost no real value. It is not enough (though it is necessary) for government to look after the casualties of the market and those who cannot be market actors. The promotion of individual autonomy and the idea that the key function of government is to 'enable' individuals by widening the range of choices available (see, e.g., Brooke 1989) presupposes that government must ensure, so far as possible, the availability to all of the things needed to be a market actor.

Saying that these are not matters of pure political choice does not mean that they are not matters of legitimate political disagreement. The issue is not one of a specific set of answers, but rather of approaching questions about the detailed how and what of public services against the background of a clear view of why public services are public. Without such an understanding, there is the danger that questions about, for example, the legitimate scope of charging, or about who counts as a 'customer', will receive answers that are inconsistent with the basic rationale for the public nature of a particular service.

Conclusion

In relation to public services, contract can never produce the automatic market processes that (in theory) operate in the private sector. This is not a defect of public services. There are good reasons, to do with the failures of markets and the rights of individuals, why public services should exist. On the other hand, these reasons themselves require that the values which underlie the symbolic appeal of contract be taken seriously and that other mechanisms and institutions be devised to ensure that those values are realized in the constitutional framework for public services.

The mechanism of contract can itself play a valuable role, within a broader legal and constitutional framework. Both accountability and individual rights can be promoted by an organizational separation of decisions as to what services there should be from the delivery of those services, and by these responsibilities being negotiated in a binding agreement between the organizations concerned. For those who see virtue only in competitive markets, this may not be enough. However, arguments that services should be private must not be confused with arguments about how best to deliver public services. The existence of such confusion and even more its deliberate promotion may facilitate developments inconsistent with the 'public service mission'. This would be a mistake since, in practice, it would lead back to the failures and evasions of ministerial responsibility. There is nothing sacrosanct about the word 'contract', but even the word is perhaps valuable. Like 'the rule of law', 'contract' is firmly attached as a label to certain important and enduring values of individual autonomy. It is the values which matter, but there is no reason to allow the word to become the exclusive property of opponents of public services.

Notes

[1] The terms 'primary', 'secondary' and later 'power-conferring' are borrowed from Hart (1961), but there is only a very loose conceptual connexion.

[2] There are other legal avenues by which individuals can bring proceedings based on failures to perform a public duty properly; e.g., nuisance, negligence, medical malpractice. Important as these remedies may be, they do not allow the individual to enforce the performance of a public duty, but only to recover damages for loss occasioned by breach of it. Of course, in the case of e.g., medical negligence, this is precisely what is required and a contractual right would add nothing.

[3] Directives in force relate to public works, (71/305/EEC as amended by Directive 89/440/EEC) and public procurement of supplies of goods and equipment (77/62/EEC, as amended by Directive 88/295/EEC). The compliance Directive (89/665/EEC) must be implemented by December 1991. A parallel set of Directives deals with contracts awarded by entities, whether publicly or privately owned, in the 'utilities' sector (energy, telecommunications, water and transport): 90/531/EEC. An equivalent of the compliance Directive ('remedies') has been proposed: COM (91) 158. A Directive on procurement of services by the utilities is under discussion: COM (91) 347.

References

Adams, John and Brownsword, Roger (1987) *Understanding Contract Law*, London, Fontana.

Adams, John and Brownsword, Roger (1990) 'Contract, consideration and the critical path', *Modern Law Review*, 53, 536-542.

Appleby, John, Robinson, Ray, Ranade, Wendy, Little, Val and Salter, Judith (1990) 'The use of markets in the health service: the NHS reforms and managed competition', *Public Money and Management*, 27-33.

Arrowsmith, Sue (1988) *Government Procurement and Judicial Review*, Toronto, Carswell.

Arrowsmith, Sue (1990) 'Judicial Review of the contractual powers of public authorities', *Law Quarterly Review*, 106, 277-292.

Assoociation of Metropolitan Authorities (1991) *Service Level Agreements: Agreeing on Quality?*, London, AMA.

Audit Commission for Local Authorities in England and Wales (1989) *Preparing for Compulsory Competition*, Occasional Paper no. 7, London, HMSO.

Berlin, Isaiah (1969) 'Two concepts of liberty' in *Four Essays on Liberty*, Oxford, Oxford University Press.

Birkinshaw, Patrick, Harden, Ian and Lewis, Norman (1990) *Government by Moonlight: the hybrid parts of the state*, London, Unwin Hyman.

Brittan, Samuel and Webb, Steven (1990) *Beyond the Welfare State: an examination of basic incomes in a market economy*, Aberdeen, Aberdeen University Press.

Brooke, Rodney (1989) *Managing the Enabling Authority*, Harlow, Longman.

Brownsword, Roger (1989) 'Liberalism and the law of contract' in Bellamy, Richard (ed.) *Liberalism and Recent Legal and Social Philosophy*: Stuttgart: Franz Steiner *Archiv für Rechts und Sozialphilosophie* Beiheft 86-100.

BSI Quality Assurance (undated) BS 5750/ISO 9000: 1987 *A Positive Contribution to better business*, BSIQA.

Carter, Neil (1991) 'Learning to measure performance: the use of indicators in organizations', *Public Administration*, 69, 85-101.

Cave, M., Hanney S., Kogan, M. and Trevitt, G. (1988) *The Use of Performance Indicators in Higher Education*, London, Jessica Kingsley.

Chartered Institute of Public Finance and Accountancy (1989) *The Audit Approach to Competition for Public Services*, London, CIPFA.

Collins, Hugh (1986) 'Contract and legal theory' in Twining, W. (ed.) *Legal Theory and Common Law*, Oxford, Blackwell.

Confederation of British Industry (1988) *The Competitive Advantage*, London, CBI.

Consumers' Association (1991) 'Public Service Compensation: a policy discussion document', London, Consumers' Association.

Crafts, Rosemary (1989) *Commissioning Health Services: contract funding in the NHS*, London, Public Finance Foundation.

Daintith, Terence (1989) 'The Executive power today' in Jowell, Jeffrey and Oliver, Dawn (eds.) *The Changing Constitution* (2nd. ed.) Oxford, Clarendon.

Davis, Kenneth, C. (1971) *Discretionary Justice: a preliminary inquiry*, Urbana, University of Chicago Press.

Department of Employment (1990) *The Management of Quality: BS 5750 and beyond*, Sheffield, Training, Enterprise and Education Division.

Department of the Environment (1988) *Competition in the Provisions* (sic) *of Local Authority Services*, Circular 19/88, London, HMSO.

Department of the Environment (1991a) *Local Government Act 1988 Part 1. Competition in the Provision of Local Authority Services*, Circular 1/91, London, HMSO.

Department of the Environment (1991b) *Local Government Review: the internal management of local authorities in England*, London, DoE.

Department of Health (1989) *Funding and Contracts for Hospital Services*, Working Paper 2, London, HMSO.

Department of Health (1990) *Contracts for Health Services: operational principles*, London, HMSO.

Department of Trade and Industry (1990) *Leadership and Quality Management: a guide for chief executives*, London, DTI.

Efficiency Unit (1988) *Improving Management in Government: the next steps*, London, HMSO.

Efficiency Unit (1991) *Making the Most of Next Steps: the management of Ministers' departments and their Executive Agencies*, London, HMSO.

Goldsworthy, Diana (1991) *Setting Up Next Steps: a short account of the origins, launch and implementation of the Next Steps Project in the British civil service*, London, HMSO.

Harden, Ian and Lewis, Norman (1986) *The Noble Lie: the British constitution and the rule of law*, London, Hutchinson.

Harden, Ian (1991) 'Review article: the constitution and its discontents', *British Journal of Political Science*, 489-510.

Harris, Neville S. (1990) 'Education by right? Breach of the duty to provide sufficient schools', *Modern Law Review*, 53, 525-536.

Hart, H. L. A. (1961) *The Concept of Law*, Oxford, Clarendon Press.

Hartley, K. (1990) 'Contracting-out in Britain: achievements and problems' in J.J. Richardson (ed.) *Privatization and De-regulation in Canada and Britain*, Aldershot, Dartmouth.

Hirschman, Albert O. (1970) *Exit, Voice and Loyalty: responses to decline in firms, organizations and states*, Cambridge, Mass., Harvard University Press.

Hughes, David (1990) 'Same story, different words?' *The Health Service Journal*, 432-4.

Hulme, Geoffrey (1990) 'Contract funding and management in the National Health Service', *Public Money and Management*, 17-23.

Jacob, Joseph M. (1991) 'Lawyers go to hospital', *Public Law*, 255-81.

Kemp, Peter (1990) 'Can the civil service adapt to managing by contract?' *Public Money and Management*, 25-31.

Levitt, M. S. and Joyce, M. A. S. (1987) *The Growth and Efficiency of Public Spending*, Cambridge, Cambridge University Press.

Lewis, N., Cracknell, S. and Seneviratne, M. (1987) *Complaints Procedures in Local Government*, Sheffield, Centre for Criminological and Socio-Legal Studies.

Lewis, N. and Harden, I., (1982) 'The Housing Corporation and "voluntary housing"' in Barker, A. (ed) *Quangos in Britain*, London, Macmillan.

Longley, D. (1990) 'Diagnostic dilemmas: accountability in the National Health Service', *Public Law,* 527-552.

Longley, D. (1992), *Public Law and Health Service Accountability*, Buckingham, Open University Press.

Marlin, John Tepper (ed.) (1984) *Contracting Municipal Services*, New York, John Wiley and Sons.

Mather, Graham (1991) *Government By Contract*, London, Institute of Economic Affairs.

National Consumer Council (1991) 'The Citizens' Charter: getting it right for the consumer', NCC PD 25/91.

NHS Management Executive (1990a) *NHS Trusts: a working guide*, London, HMSO.

NHS Management Executive (1990b) *Contracts for Health Services: operating contracts*, London, HMSO.

NHS Management Executive (1991) 'NHS Contracts: Guidance on Resolving Disputes', letter dated 5th March 1991 reference EL (91) 11.

OFTEL (1989) 'British Telecom's contract terms and conditions for telephone services', Statement dated 6th March 1989.

Pirie, Madsen (1991) *The Citizens' Charter*, London, Adam Smith Institute.

Pirie, Madsen, Mather, Graham, Freeman, David and Monckton, Christopher (1991) *Empowerment*, London, ASI (Research) Limited.

Poggi, Gianfranco (1978) *The Development of the Modern State*, London, Hutchinson.

Price Waterhouse (1991) *Executive Agencies: facts and trends*, 3rd. ed. London, Price Waterhouse.

Ragnemalm, Hans (1991) 'The Ombudsman', unpublished paper to seminar of the European Commission for Democracy through Law.

Reich, Charles (1964) 'The new property', *Yale Law Journal,* 73, 773-787.

Rose, Richard (1990) 'Charging for public services', *Public Administration*, 68, 297-313.

Smith, B. L. R. and Hague, D. C. (1971) *The Dilemma of Accountability in Modern Government: independence versus control*, London, Macmillan.

Stewart, Richard (1975) 'The reformation of American administrative law', *Harvard Law Review*, 88, 1667-1813.

Treasury (1986) *Using Private Enterprise in Government: report of a multi-departmental review of competitive tendering and contracting for services in government departments,* London, HMSO.

Treasury (1988a) *Public Purchasing Policy: Consolidated Guidelines*, London, HM Treasury.

Treasury (1988b) *Guidance Notes on Public Sector Purchasing International Obligations: Supplies Contracts*, London, HM Treasury.

Treasury (1990) *Guidance on the EC Works Directive*, London, HM Treasury.

Treasury and Civil Service Committee (1988) Eighth Report 1987/88 *Civil Service Management Reform: the Next Steps*, vol II HC 494-II, London, HMSO.

Treasury and Civil Service Committee (1990) Eighth Report 1989/90 *Progress in the Next Steps Initiative*, HC 481, London, HMSO.

Turpin, Colin (1989) *Government Procurement and Contracts*, Harlow, Longman.

Walsh, Kieron (1991) *Competitive Tendering for Local Authority Services: initial experiences*, London, HMSO.

Command Papers

Cmnd 218, *Report of the Committee on Administrative Tribunals and Enquiries*, 1957.

Cmnd 3638, *The Civil Service*, 1968.

Cmnd 9058, *Financial Management in Government Departments*, 1983.

Cm 524 *Civil Service Management Reform: the Next Steps, Government reply to the 8th Report from the Treasury and Civil Service Committee, session 1987-88, HC 494-I*, 1988.

Cm 841, *Developments in the Next Steps Programme*, 1989.

Cm 914, *The Financing and Accountability of Next Steps Agencies*, 1989.

Cm 1263, *Progress in the Next Steps Initiative*, 1990.

Cm 1599, *The Citizen's Charter: raising the standard*, 1991.